Benjamin Franklin, Humphry Marshall

Arbustrum Americanum

The American Grove

Benjamin Franklin, Humphry Marshall

Arbustrum Americanum
The American Grove

ISBN/EAN: 9783337225735

Printed in Europe, USA, Canada, Australia, Japan

Cover: Foto ©Suzi / pixelio.de

More available books at **www.hansebooks.com**

ARBUSTRUM AMERICANUM:

THE

AMERICAN GROVE,

OR, AN

ALPHABETICAL CATALOGUE

OF

FOREST TREES AND *SHRUBS*,

NATIVES OF THE AMERICAN UNITED STATES,

ARRANGED ACCORDING TO THE LINNÆAN SYSTEM.

CONTAINING,

The particular diſtinguiſhing *Characters* of each GENUS, with plain, ſimple and familiar *Deſcriptions* of the *Manner* of *Growth*, *Appearance*, *&c.* of their ſeveral SPECIES and VARIETIES.

ALSO, SOME HINTS OF THEIR USES IN

MEDICINE, DYES, AND DOMESTIC OECONOMY.

COMPILED FROM ACTUAL KNOWLEDGE AND OBSERVATION, AND THE ASSISTANCE OF BOTANICAL AUTHORS,

BY HUMPHRY MARSHALL.

PHILADELPHIA:

PRINTED BY JOSEPH CRUKSHANK, IN MARKET-STREET, BETWEEN SECOND AND THIRD-STREETS.

M DCC LXXXV.

TO

BENJAMIN FRANKLIN, Esquire,

PRESIDENT,

JOHN EWING, D. D.
WILLIAM WHITE, D. D. and } *Vice-Presidents,*
SAMUEL VAUGHAN, Esquire,

AND

TO THE OTHER MEMBERS

OF THE

AMERICAN PHILOSOPHICAL SOCIETY,

THIS

ALPHABETICAL CATALOGUE

OF THE

FOREST TREES AND SHRUBS,

NATIVES *of the* AMERICAN UNITED STATES,

IS RESPECTFULLY DEDICATED

By the Author.

INTRODUCTION.

WHEN we take a ſurvey of Mankind in general, and of the ſeveral requiſites by which life is rendered comfortable and deſirable, the productions of the Vegetable Kingdom are amongſt the foremoſt; as affording the principal neceſſaries, conveniencies, and luxuries of life.

It is in this view, that the Science of Botany, or that branch of natural Hiſtory which teaches the right knowledge of Vegetables, and their application to the moſt beneficial uſes, is an object which not only merits the attention and encouragement of every patriotic and liberal mind, but undoubtedly deſerves a place amongſt the firſt of uſeful purſuits. That it is an object highly deſerving the attention of Mankind in general, cannot be denied; but in a particular manner of the inhabitants of this Commonwealth, the author wiſhes to make appear more obvious.

Thoſe who are converſant in trade well know the continual enormous expence we are at in purchaſing foreign Teas, Drugs, Dye-ſtuffs, &c. The diminution of this, ought to be the care and concern of every friend to his Country's welfare. And we preſume it will appear evident, that the moſt eligible and obvious

means

means of obtaining this desirable object, will be by a proper attention and application to Horticulture and Botany. In this view, the following considerations more particularly present themselves.

I. *The introduction and cultivation of foreign useful and valuable plants.* Our extent of territory, our diversity of Climate, of Soil, and of Stuation, leaves not a doubt but that we might introduce and cultivate to advantage, many of the same articles, whose importation at this time, is to us, a considerable expence. The *Thea viridis* & *bohea*, the true green and bohea Tea plant, formerly accounted different species, but now known to be the same, and one of the greatest drainers of our wealth; may be procured either from its native place of growth, or from Europe where it has become pretty common; and we have every reason to believe, from its being the spontaneous produce of the same parallel of latitude, and from other considerations respecting its natural history, that it might thrive well in our Southern States. In this same view the Vine, the Almond Tree, Fig Tree, Liquorice, Madder and Rhubarb, deservedly require our attention. Many other* foreign useful plants might be enumerated, and the advantages that may be derived to this Commonwealth from their introduction, encrease and culture, must appear sufficiently obvious.

* See Transactions of the American Philosophical Society, Vol. I. Page 155.

II. *The diſcovering the qualities and uſes of our own native Vegetable productions, and applying them to the moſt uſeful purpoſes.* Our extent of luxuriant unexplored territory, is an object which here in a particular manner occurs replete with promiſing advantages. Our being able to diſcover a plant of equal general uſage with the *Potatoe*, *Tobacco*, or *Ginſeng;* or good ſubſtitutes for *Tea*, *Coffee* and *Peruvian Bark;* would be advantages ſurpaſſing all adequate eſtimation.

It is true, we may gain by tedious experience, or ſtumble by chance upon many uſeful diſcoveries reſpecting the uſes and medicinal virtues of plants, but it is from our obſervations and reſearches founded upon, and directed by, a *knowledge of Botany*, that we can alone hope for certain ſucceſs. From the writings of the celebrated LINNÆUS this general rule is ſufficiently eſtabliſhed; that plants of the ſame habit and appearance, and thoſe which agree in the diſpoſition of their flowers and fruit, have likewiſe ſimilar virtues and properties. From this obſervation we deduce an obvious inference; that the more general knowledge we obtain of the characters and appearance of plants, the more likely we ſhall be alſo to encreaſe our knowledge of their virtues, qualities and uſes.

This ſubject has been much urged and long dwelt upon from a conviction of its importance and promiſing advantages: the author, influenced by theſe conſiderations, and from a belief a belief that it might contribute in ſome degree to render a knowledge of this ſubject more familiar and eaſy, has been induced to draw up this Alphabetical Catalogue of the Foreſt Trees and Shrubs, natives of the American United States, as mentioned by the beſt authors, or ſince diſcovered by ingenious travellers. In this Catalogue are contained their Linnæan Generic and trivial names, (or new formed ones where theſe have been wanting) together with their moſt common and approved Engliſh ones; the particular diſtinguiſhing characters of each Genus; a plain and familiar deſcription of the appearance, manner of growth, &c. of their ſeveral ſpecies and varieties; and alſo, ſome hints of their native ſoil and ſituation, uſes in Medicine, as Dyes and in domeſtic œconomy.

As terms peculiar to the ſcience frequently and unavoidably occur, it was judged neceſſary, in order to render the work more uſeful and complete, to prefix a general explanation of the Linnæan ſyſtem of arrangement, as alſo of the uſeful and unavoidable ſcientific terms; for this and other purpoſes the author has availed himſelf from the beſt writers, of what has been judged moſt applicable and conducive to his deſign. The whole forming an uſeful *Vademecum Botanicum*, or Botanical Companion.

In this my *Countrymen* are preſented at one view with a conciſe deſcription of their own native Foreſt Trees and Shrubs, as far as hitherto diſcovered. And thoſe whoſe fancy

may

may lead to this delightful ſcience, may by a little application, from hence be enabled ſcientifically to examine and arrange, not only thoſe of the ſhrubby, but the ſeveral and various ſpecies of the herbaceous claſs. The *foreigner*, curious in American collections, will be hereby better enabled to make a ſelection ſuitable to his own particular fancy. If he wiſhes to cultivate timber for œconomical purpoſes, he is here informed of our valuable Foreſt Trees: if for adorning his plantation or garden of our different ornamental flowering ſhrubs.

The author would have been happy, could he have given alſo a deſcriptive Catalogue of our native herbaceous plants. At preſent, circumſtances oblige him to confine himſelf to Foreſt Trees and Shrubs; however he has ſuch a work in contemplation ſhould this meet with the encouragement of the public.

He is well aware that many improvements might have been made, with regard to the form and manner of deſcription, as well as by the addition of Synonyms, Notes of reference, &c. but, upon reflecting that the generality of his Readers would have been more embarraſſed and confuſed than profited thereby, he was determined to uſe the moſt plain and familiar method and language, in order to render the work as generally uſeful as poſſible; this being the chief end and deſign of the undertaking.

A View of the Twenty-four Classes of the SEXUAL SYSTEM *of* LINNÆUS, *with their Names and Characters; also the Numberand Explanation of Orders contained in each.*

Number of the Classes.	*Their Names and Characters.*	*Number of Orders in each.*	*Their Names, expressive of the Number of Female Parts or Styles.*	*Number.*
1.	MONANDRIA. One fertile stamen, i. e. having the *Antheræ.*	2	1. Monogynia, - -	1
			2. Digynia, - - -	2
2.	DIANDRIA. Two fruitful *Stamina* or male parts.	3	1. Monogynia, - -	1
			2. Digynia, - - -	2
			3. Trigynia, - -	3
3.	TRIANDRIA. Three ditto.	3	1. Monogynia, - -	1
			2. Digynia, - -	2
			3. Trigynia, - -	3
4.	TETRANDRIA. Four ditto, all of equal length, by which it is distinguished from the fourteenth class.	3	1. Monogynia, - -	1
			2. Digynia, - - -	2
			3. Tetragynia, - -	4
5.	PENTANDRIA. Six ditto.	6	1. Monogynia, - -	1
			2. Digynia, - - -	2
			3. Triginia, - -	3
			4. Tetragynia, - -	4
			5. Pentagynia, - -	5
			6. Polygynia, - -	many
6.	HEXANDRIA. Six ditto, all of equal length, by which this is distinguished from the sixteenth class.	5	1. Monogynia, - -	1
			2. Digynia, - - -	2
			3. Trigynia, - -	3
			4. Tetragynia, -	4
			5. Polygynia, - -	many
7.	HEPTANDRIA. Seven ditto.	4	1. Monogynia, - -	1
			2. Digynia, -	2
			3. Tetragynia, - -	4
			4. Heptagynia, -	7
8.	OCTANDRIA. Eight ditto.	4	1. Monogynia, - -	1
			2. Digynia, - -	2
			3. Trigynia, - -	3
			4. Tetragynia, -	4
9.	ENNEANDRIA. Nine ditto.	3	1. Monogynia, - -	1
			2. Trigynia, - -	2
			3. Hexagynia, - -	6

10. DECAN-

Number of the Classes.	Their Names and Characters.	Number of Orders in each.	Their Names, expressive of the Number of Female Parts or Styles.	Number.
10.	DECANDRIA. Ten ditto.	5	1. Monogynia,	1
			2. Digynia,	2
			3. Trigynia,	3
			4. Pentagynia,	5
			5. Decagynia,	10
11.	DODECANDRIA. From eleven to nineteen *Stamina*, inclusive.	6	1. Monogynia,	1
			2. Digynia,	2
			3. Trigynia	3
			4. Pentagynia,	5
			5. Octagynia,	8
			6. Dodecagynia,	12
12.	ICOSANDRIA. Twenty stamina and upwards (sometimes fewer) affixed to the inner side of the *Corolla* or calyx and not to the receptacle; the corolla is fastened to the inner side of the calyx, which is concave and of one leaf.	5	1. Monogynia,	1
			2. Digynia,	2
			3. Trigynia,	3
			4. Pentagynia,	5
			5. Polygynia,	many
13.	POLYANDRIA. From fifteen to one thousand stamina, which are fastened to the receptacle. It differs from the *Icosandria* in the calyx and the insertion of the *Stamina* and *Corolla*.	7	1. Monogynia,	1
			2. Digynia,	2
			3. Trigynia,	3
			4. Tetragynia,	4
			5. Pentagynia,	5
			6. Hexagynia,	6
			7. Polygynia,	many

			Their Names expressive of the disposition of their Seeds.
14.	DIDYNAMIA. Four *Stamina*: the two next to one another shorter than the other two; one style and an uneven *Corolla*.	2	1. Gymnospermia---Seeds naked in the calyx.
			2. Angiospermia----Seeds covered in a seed-vessel.
15.	TETRADYNAMIA. Six *Stamina*, tapering and erect: the two opposite as long as the calyx, the other four a little longer; four even petals.	2	1. Siliculosa--Seeds in small short pods.
			2. Siliquosa---Seeds in long slender pods.

16. MONA-

Number of the Claſſes.	*Their Names and Characters.*	*Number of Orders in each.*	*Their Names chiefly expreſſive of the Number of Male Parts or Stamina.*	*Number.*
16.	MONADELPHIA. A *Perianthium*, permanent, often double; five petals. The filaments all joined in one parcel below, but not above; the external ſhorteſt.	5	1. Pentandria, - -	5
			2. Decandria, - - -	10
			3. Endecandria, - -	11
			4. Dodecandria, - -	12
			5. Polyandria, - -	many
17.	DIADELPHIA. The filaments all joined below in two parcels, one ſimple the other nine-cleft. A perianthium of one leaf, bell-ſhaped and falling-off. The *Corolla* always butter-fly-ſhaped and uneven.	3	1. Hexandria, - -	6
			2. Octandria, - - -	8
			3. Decandria, - -	10
18.	POLYADELPHIA. The filaments united below into three or more diſtinct parcels.	3	1. Pentandria, - - -	5
			2. Icoſandria, -	20
			3. Polyandria, -	many
19.	SYNGENESIA. The *Stamina* joined by their *Antheræ* (rarely by their filaments) in form of a cylinder.	6	1. Polygamia Æqualis---- Equal Polygamy. The florets all hermaphrodite.	
			2. Polygamia Superflua--- Superfluous Polygamy. The florets in the center hermaphrodite, thoſe in the circumference female.	
			3. Polygamia Fruſtanea--- Ineffectual Polygamy. The florets in the center hermaphrodite, thoſe in the circumference barren.	
			4. Polygamia Neceſſaria--- Neceſſary Polygamy. The hermaphrodite florets in the center barren, but the female in the circumference fruitful.	
			5. Polygamia Segregata--- Separate Polygamy. The florets ſeparated by partial flower-cups within a common calyx.	
			6. Monogamia, Single marriages, containing ſimple flowers whoſe Antheræ are united.	

Number of the Classes.	*Their Names and Characters.*	*Number of Orders in each.*	*Their Names chiefly expressive of the Number of Male Parts or Stamina.*	*Number.*
20.	GYNANDRIA. The *Stamina* or male parts attached to, and growing upon the female or *Pistillum.*	7	1. Diandria,	2
			2. Triandria,	3
			3. Tetrandria,	4
			4. Pentandria,	5
			5. Hexandria,	6
			6. Decandria,	10
			7. Polyandria,	many
21.	MONOECIA. Male and female flowers in distinct cups on the same plant.	11	1. Monandria,	1
			2. Diandria,	2
			3. Triandria,	3
			4. Tetrandria,	4
			5. Pentandria,	5
			6. Hexandria,	6
			7. Heptandria,	7
			8. Polyandria,	many
			9. Monadelphia, Filaments united.	
			10. Syngenesia, Antheræ united.	
			11. Gynandria, Stamina growing out of the pistillum.	
22.	DIOECIA. Male and female flowers on different plants of the same Species.	14	1. Monandria.	1
			2. Diandria,	2
			3. Triandria,	3
			4. Tetrandria,	4
			5. Pentandria,	5
			6. Hexandria,	6
			7. Octandria,	7
			8. Enneandria,	8
			9. Decandria,	10
			10. Dodecandria,	12
			11. Polyandria,	many
			12. Monadelphia, Filaments united.	
			13. Diadelphia, Antheræ united.	
			14. Syngenesia, Stamina growing out of the pistillum.	
23.	POLYGAMIA. Male, female and hermaphrodite flowers distinct in the same Species, and sometimes on the same plant.	3	1. Monoecia, one house, or male and female flowers on the same plant.	
			2. Dioecia, two houses, or male and female flowers on separate plants.	
			3. Trioecia, three houses, or male, female and hermaphrodite, growing on three distinct plants of the same Genus.	
24.	CRYPTOGAMIA. The fructification either wholly escapes our notice, or the flowers are hid within the fruit.	4	1. Filices. Ferns.	
			2. Musci. Mosses.	
			3. Algæ. Fucus, or Sea-weed.	
			4. Fungi, Mushrooms.	

Note, *Palmæ*, the Palms have, in late works, been added by way of appendix, and constitutes the 25th class; but as these are not natives of these States, and their fructification but imperfectly known, they are omitted.

From the preceding View it appears, that the Names and Characters of the Twenty-four Classes, are each founded on either the *Number*, *Insertion*, *Equality*, *Connection*, *Situation*, or *Absence* of the STAMINA or MALE SEXUAL ORGANS.

On Number only, are founded the first eleven Classes, from Monandria to Dodecandria.

On Number and Insertion, } Icosandria and Polyandria.

On Number and Equality, } Didynamia and Tetradynamia.

On Connection, Monadelphia, Diadelphia, Polyadelphia, and Syngenesia.

On Insertion only, Gynandria.

On Situation, Monoecia, Dioecia and Polygamia.

On Absence, Cryptogamia.

An Explanation of the different parts of Fructification.

FRUCTIFICATION is a temporary part of vegetables, appointed for the purpofe of generation, terminating the old vegetable and beginning the new. The parts of fructification are the feven following, viz.

1. The *Calyx*, flower-cup, or empalement.
2. The *Corolla*, petals, or painted leaves of the flower.
3. The *Stamina*, threads, or chives.
4. The *Piftilum*, or pointal.
5. The *Pericarpium*, or Seed-veffel.
6. The *Seeds*.
7. The *Receptacle*, or bafe on which all the other parts of the fructification are connected.

I. The *calyx* (which is the termination of the outer bark of the plant, prefenting itfelf in the fructification, in this form) comprehends the feven following fpecies, viz. the *perianthium*, the *involucrum*, the *amentum*, the *fpadix*, the *gluma*, the *calyptra*, and *volva*, of each of which in their order.

1. The *perianthium*, the flower-cup or empalement properly fo called, is the moft common fpecies of calyx, and fituated clofe to the fructification. If it enclofes the *ftamina* and *germen*, it is called the *perianthium* of the fructification. If it enclofes the *Stamina* and not the *germen*, it is the *perianthium* of the flower. If it includes the *germem*, and not the *ftamina*, it is the *perianthium* of the fruit.
2. The *involucrum* or cover is fituated at the bottom of an umbel, at fome diftance from the flower. It is called an univerfal *involucrum* or cover, if it is fituated at the bottom of an univerfal umbel; and a partial *involucrum* or cover, if at the foot of a partial umbel.
3. The *amentum* or katkin is that fort of calyx, which confifts of a great number of chaffy fcales proceeding from a common receptacle or flender thread, as in hazel, alder, &c.
4. The *fpatha* or fheath is a fort of calyx which burfts lengthways, and puts forth a ftalk fupporting the flowers; as in *narciffus*, fnow-drop, *arum*, indian turnep &c.
5. The *gluma* or chaffy hufk, is that fort of calyx peculiar to graffes, compofed of thin fcales or valves, which are often terminated by an *arifta*, a beard, or awn.
6. The *calyptra* a veil or hood, is a fort of calyx peculiar to

mofles,

moſſes, placed over their *antheræ*, and reſembling a monk's cowl, or rather an extinguiſher.

7. The *volva* is a ſort of calyx peculiar to the *fungi* or muſhroom tribe, involving or incloſing their fructification. It is membranaceous and torn quite round.

II. The *corolla*, literally a wreath or garland, (ſerving together with the calyx as covers to the parts they incloſe) is the termination of the inner bark of the plant preſenting itſelf in this form, and conſiſts of the *petalum* and *nectarium*.

1. The *petalum* or petal is the corrollaceous covering of the flower. If the flower is monopetalous, *i. e.* conſiſts of one petal, the lower hollow part of ſuch a *corolla* is called *tubus*, the tube, and the upper part which ſpreads wider is called *limbus*, the limb or border. And from its different figure it is called either,

Bell-ſhaped, without any tube below,
Funnel-ſhaped or conical, with a tube,
Saucer or *ſalver-ſhaped*, with a tube,
Wheel-ſhaped, without any tube below; or
Gaping, lipped or maſked.

If the *corrolla* be polypetalous, *i. e.* conſiſts of many petals, the lower part of each petal is called, the *unguis*, or claw.

And the upper part which is wider, is called the *lamina*, or thin plate.

Again this upper part or *lamina*, is either

Croſſ-ſhaped, of four equal ſpreading petals; or

Butter-fly-ſhaped, irregular and of four petals; the upper one of which is called the *ſtandard*; the two ſide ones *wings*; and the under one the *keel*.

2. The *nectarium* is that part of the corolla which contains the honey; having a wonderful variety both as to ſhape and ſituation, and is ſometimes united with the petals, and ſometimes ſeparate from them.

III. The *ſtamina* are thoſe parts of a flower appropriated to the preparation of the *pollen*, or fecundating duſt, and conſiſt of the *filamentum*, the *anthera*, and the *pollen*.

1. The *filamentum*, the filament or thread ſerves to elevate the *antheræ*, and connect it to the flower.

2. The *anthera*, or ſummit of the *ſtamen*, is that part which contains the *pollen* or fecundating duſt, and diſcharges it when ripe.

3. The *pollen*, or impregnating duſt, is that fine powder contained within the *antheræ*, or tops of the ſtamina, and diſperſed when ripe, upon the female organ, for impregnating the ſame.

IV. The

IV. The *piſtillum*, pointal, or female organ, adheres to the fruit, and is that part appropriated for the reception of the *pollen*, ſpoken of above. . It conſiſts of the *germen*, the *ſtylus*, and the *ſtigma*.

1. The *germen*, or ſeed-bud, is the baſe or lower part of the *piſtillum*, containing the rudiments of the unripe fruit, or ſeed, in the flowering ſtate of the plant,

2. The *ſtylus*, or ſtyle, is that part of the *piſtillum* which ſtands upon the *germen*, and elevates the *ſtigma* or ſummit.

3. The *ſtigma*, the ſummit, or top of the ſtyle, is that part which receives the fertilizing duſt of the *antheræ*, and tranſmits its *effluvia*, through the ſtyle into the middle of the *germen*, or ſeed-bud.

V. The *pericarpium*, or ſeed veſſel, is that part which contains the ſeeds, and diſcharges them when ripe. It comprehends the eight following ſpecies, viz. the *capſula*, the *ſiliqua*, the *legumen*, the *conceptaculum* or *folliculus*, the *drupa*, the *pomum*, the *bacca*, and the *ſtrobilus*; of each of which in their order.

1. The *capſula*, a capſule or little caſket, is a dry hollow ſeed-veſſel, that ſplits or opens in ſome determinate manner. Capſules, when opened or ſplit, are divided outwardly into one or more pieces, called *valvulæ*, or valves, the parts which divide the capſules internally into cells are called *diſſepimenta*, or partitions. And the ſubſtances which connect the partitions to the ſeeds, are called *columellæ*, or little-pillars. The empty ſpaces for containing the ſeeds, are called *loculamenta*, or cells.

2. The *ſiliqua*, or pod is a ſeed-veſſel with two valves, having the ſeeds fixed along the joining or edge of both valves.

3. The *legumen*, or cod, is a ſeed-veſſel with two valves, having the ſeeds fixed along the edge of one of the valves only.

4. The *conceptaculum*, a receiver; or *folliculus*, a little bag, is a ſeed-veſſel with one valve, ſplitting length-ways from top to bottom, and has no ſeam for faſtening the ſeeds within it.

5. The *drupa*, drupe, or ſtone fruit, is a pulpy ſeed-veſſel, which has no valve, or external opening, and contains within it a ſtone or nut.

6. The *pomum*, or apple, is a pulpy ſeed-veſſel, which has no valve or external opening, and contains within it a capſule.

7. The *bacca*, or berry, is a pulpy ſeed veſſel, which has no valve, and contains ſeeds which are naked, or have no other covering than the pulp.

8. The

8. The *ſtrobilus*, or cone, is a ſeed-veſſel compoſed of woody ſcales, laid over one another like tiles; it opens only at top, the ſcales being fixed below to the center of the cone.

VI. *Semen*, the ſeed, is a deciduous part of the plant, containing the rudiments of a new vegetable, and fertilized by the ſprinkling of the male duſt. Under this head are comprehended the ſeed properly ſo called, the *nut* and *propago*.

The *nut* is a ſeed covered with a hard bony ſkin.

Propago, the ſeed of the moſſes, which has no tunic or covering.

VII. The *receptaculum*, or receptacle, the ſeventh and laſt part of the fructification on which the other ſix are connected, comprehends the *receptaculum proprium*, the *receptaculum commune*, and the *ſpadix*.

1. The *receptaculum proprium*, or proper receptacle, which belongs to the parts of a ſingle fructification only. It is called the receptacle either of the *fructification*, when it is common to both flower and fruit; of the *flower*, when the parts of the flower only are faſtened to it without the *germen*; of the *fruit* when it is a baſe for the fruit, and at a diſtance from the receptacle of the flower; or of the *ſeeds*, when it is a baſe to which the ſeeds are fixed within the *pericarpium* or ſeed-veſſel.

2. The *receptaculum commune*, or common receptacle, is that which connects ſeveral florets together; as in compound flowers; and is either *paleaceum* chaffy, *i. e.* with thin membranaceous chaffy plates riſing between the florets, or *nudum* naked, without chaffy plates.

3. The *ſpadix* is the receptacle of the palms, and is always branched. It is alſo uſed to ſignify the flower ſtalk of every plant, which was originally contained within a *ſpatha* or ſheath; but in this laſt caſe it is often ſimple.

Explanation of the Modes of Flowering.

The *peduncle* or foot-ſtalk of the flower is a partial trunk, bearing the fructification only, but not the leaves.

When branched or divided, each of the diviſions is called *pedicellus*, or a little flower-ſtalk.

Flower-ſtalks are diſtinguiſhed from the place of the plant where they grow, into,

1. The *radical* flower-ſtalk, when they proceed immediately from the root.
2. The *cauline* flower-ſtalk, which proceeds from the ſtem.

3. The

3. The *branch* peduncle, which proceeds from the branches.
4. The *axillary*, or bofom flower-ftalk, which comes out be tween the leaf and ftem, or between the branch and ftem.
5. The *terminal* flower-ftalk, which comes from the extremity of the branch or ftem.
6. The *folitary* peduncle, when there is only one in the fame place.
7. The *fcattered* peduncles, when a great many grow together without any order.

Flower-ftalks are alfo diftinguifhed from the different modes in which flowers are borne and connected on them, into the *uniflorous*, *biflorous*, *triflorous*, or *multiflorous* peduncle, that is, which bear one, two, three, or many flowers.

Flowers are alfo collected or borne in the ten following modes.

1. The *fafciculus*, a bunch or bundle, when peduncles are erect, parallel, placed clofe to one another, and all of the fame height, as in *fweet-william*.
2. The *capitulum*, a little head, where many flowers are collected into a head, at the extremity of a peduncle, as in *globe amaranthus*.
3. The *fpike*, where the flowers fit clofe without foot-ftalks, and are placed along a common flower-ftalk. A fpike is called *fecunda*, fingle ranked, when all the flowers are turned to one fide; or *difticha*, double ranked, when the flowers look to both fides, or ftand two ways.
4. The *corymbus*, where the leffer flower-ftalks of unequal lengths are produced along the common peduncle on all fides, and rife to the fame height, fo as to form a flat or even furface at top, as in *fpiræa opulifolia*.
5. The *panicle* where the fructifications are difperfed upon foot-ftalks varioufly fubdivided, as in oats, &c. a panicle is faid to be *diffufe* when the partial foot-ftalks diverge, and the fructifications hang loofe; or *ftraight* and narrow; when the foot-ftalks approach near to one another.
6. The *thyrfus* is a panicle contracted into an oval or egg-fhaped-form, fomewhat refembling the cone of a pine; as in *lilac*, *horfe chefnut*, &c.
7. The *racemus* or clufter, confifts of a common peduncle, having fhort lateral branches, all nearly of equal length proceeding from it; as in the *vine*, *currants* &c. It is called *racemus fecundus*, or a one ranked clufter when all the foot-ftalks incline to one fide; as in the *forrel-tree* and moft of our *andromedas*.

1. The

8. The *verticillus*, or whorl, where the flowers are produced in rings at each joint of the ſtem, with very ſhort foot-ſtalks; as in *mint*, *horehound*, &c.
9. The *umbella* or umbel, where a number of ſmall flower-ſtalks riſe from the ſame center to an equal height and form an even ſurface at top. It is called a *ſimple umbel*, when the flower-ſtalks are ſimple or undivided; and a *compound umbel*, or ſometimes an *univerſal umbel*, when all the foot-ſtalks are ſubdivided into ſmaller umbels, commonly called *partial umbels*
10. The *cyma*, or irregular umbel, where the foot-ſtalks riſe from a common center, and to an equal height, as in the umbel; but the ſecondary or partial foot-ſtalks are irregularly diſperſed, without order as in *elder*, *viburnum* &c.

☞ *The Reader is requeſted to obſerve that the names of the Species, under which the words,* Bartram's Catalogue *immediately occur, are not found in Linnæus's Species Plantarum, but are taken from a Sheet Catalogue publiſhed by John and William Bartram, Botaniſts in Kingſeſſing; containing the names of Foreſt Trees and Shrubs, growing in, or near their Garden.*

A CAT.

A CATALOGUE OF TREES AND SHRUBS.

ACER.

THE MAPLE TREE.

Clafs 23, Order 1. Polyandria Monoecia.

IT hath Hermaphrodite and Male flowers upon the fame tree.

In the *Hermaphrodite*,

The *Empalement* is of one leaf, five cleft, acute, coloured, plain and entire at the bafe, and permanent.

The *Corolla* confifts of five petals, which are ovate, broader outward, obtufe, fcarce larger than the calyx, and fpreading.

The *Filaments* are eight, awl-fhaped and fhort. The *Antheræ* fimple.

The *Germen* is compreffed and funk in the Receptacle, which is large, convex and perforated. The *Style* is thread-form, encreafing in length. The *Stigmas* two, fharp-pointed, flender, and reflexed.

The *Seed-veffels* are two capfules joined at the bafe, roundifh, compreffed, and each terminating in a large membranaceous wing.

The *Seeds* are folitary and roundifh.

The *Male* are the fame in all parts except wanting the germen and ftyle.

Obf. The Afh-leaved Maple has male and female flowers on feparate trees.

The Species *with us are,*

1. ACER pennſylvanicum----*Pennſylvanian Dwarf Mountain Maple.*

This grows naturally upon the mountains in the back parts of Pennſylvania. The ſtems are ſlender, riſing to the height of ſix or eight feet, and ſending off ſeveral oppoſite branches. The leaves are three-pointed, pretty much ſawed on their edges, and placed oppoſite upon pretty long footſtalks. The flowers terminate the ſtalks in a pretty long erect *racemus* or bunch; they are ſmall, of an herbaceous colour, and in part ſucceeded by ſmall conjoined winged ſeeds.

2. ACER glaucum. *The Silver-leaved Maple.*

This tree grows frequently to the height of fifty or ſixty feet, with many ſpreading branches. The leaves are five-lobed, ſomewhat toothed, or deeply and irregularly ſawed on their edges: they are of a lucid green on the upper ſide and a bright ſilver colour on their under. The flowers are produced in little umbels at the foot of the leaves; they are of a deep red colour, and are ſucceeded by large winged ſeeds, which fall off early in the ſummer. This is perhaps the Acer rubrum of Linnæus.

3. ACER Negundo. *The Aſh-leaved Maple.*

This tree is dioecious, or having male and female flowers upon different trees; it is but of middling growth, riſing perhaps to the height of twenty or thirty feet. The leaves ſomething reſemble thoſe of the Aſh, but are generally trifoliate or quinquefoliate, or conſiſting of three or five lobes; which are oval, ſomewhat pointed, and a little notched towards their extremities. The flowers of the male are produced

upon

upon pendulous bundles of very long fine threads or footſtalks, each having a ſmall flower-cup at its extremity, containing five or more ſtamina. The female produces flowers at the extremity of the ſmall branches, in long looſe bunches; they have long footſtalks, with a ſmall deciduous empalement; containing a compreſſed germen, with ſcarce any ſtyle, but two reflexed ſtigmas.

4. ACER canadenſe. *American ſtriped Maple.*

This is but of middling growth. The bark, eſpecially of the young ſhoots, is beautifully variegated or ſtriped. The leaves are divided into three very ſharp pointed lobes, and very finely ſawed on their edges. The flowers are produced in ſolitary bunches, with ſhortiſh footſtalks; having pretty large petals and empalements, containing generally eight ſtamina or filaments; and in hermaphrodite flowers two reflexed ſtigmas. The flowers and ſeeds are of a greeniſh yellow colour.

5. ACER rubrum. *The Scarlet flowering Maple.*

This grows to a pretty large ſize in a rich ſoil. The leaves are three and ſometimes nearly five lobed, and ſawed on their edges. The flowers are produced in little umbels cloſely ſurrounding the ſmall branches, and are of a ſcarlet colour. The footſtalks of the hermaphrodite flowers, ſhoot out to a conſiderable length; they are of a ſcarlet colour, each ſuſtaining two joined winged ſeeds, ſomewhat of the ſame colour. There is a variety of this with yellowiſh flowers and ſeeds, which is, I believe, the moſt common kind in Pennſylvania.

6. ACER

6. Acer saccharum. *The Sugar Maple.*

This grows to a large tree of two feet or more in diameter, and fifty or sixty feet high. The leaves something resemble the Silver-leaved Maple, but are not so large, nor deeply lobed; or of so fine a silver colour. It flowers in manner of the Scarlet Maple, but the flowers are of an herbaceous colour; and produces large joined winged seeds. The back inhabitants make a pretty good sugar, and in considerable quantity, of the sap of this and the Silver-leaved Maple; and though these have generally been preferred, yet all our Maples yield a sap which affords a pretty good sugar.

ÆSCULUS.

THE HORSE-CHESNUT-TREE.

Class 7. Order 1. Heptandria Monogynia.

THE *Empalement* is of one leaf, tubulous, small and five-toothed.

The *Corolla* consists of five petals, roundish, waved with a plaited margin, plane, spreading, unequally coloured, and inserted by narrow claws into the calyx.

The *Filaments* are seven (sometimes eight) awl-shaped, the length of the corolla, and declined. The *Antheræ* rising.

The *Germen* is roundish, ending in an awl-shaped *Style*. The *Stigma* sharp pointed.

The *Seed-vessel* a capsule, coriaceous, roundish, three-cell'd and three valv'd.

The *Seeds* or nuts two, somewhat globose, often but one arriving to perfection.

1. Æsculus octandra. *New river Horse Chesnut.*

This often becomes a tree of pretty large size. The branches are smooth and of a greyish colour. The leaves are palmated, or composed of five pretty large

large lobes joined at their baſe, having a pretty long common footſtalk: they are ſomewhat wedge ſhape, or narrower towards the baſe than the point, veined with oblique parallel veins, and ſawed on their edges. The flowers are produced in a looſe *thyrſus*, at the extremity of the branches, of a pale yellowiſh colour; and are ſucceeded by fruit near the ſize of the eaſtern Horſe-Cheſnut.

2. ÆSCULUS Pavia. *Scarlet flowering Horſe-Cheſnut.*

This is but of humble growth, ſeldom riſing to more than ten or twelve feet high; ſending out ſeveral branches, with leaves and flowers much like the former, except the flowers being of a bright red colour: they ſtand upon ſhort naked footſtalks, branching from the common ſtem, generally five or ſix together in each *thyrſus*. They are tubulous at bottom but ſpread open at top, where the petals are irregular in ſize and length, having ſomething the appearance of a lip flower; they have ſeven or eight ſtamina the length of the petals. When the flower fades the Germen ſwells to a pear ſhaped fruit, with a thick ruſſet coloured covering, containing ſometimes one or two nuts.

AMORPHA.

BASTARD-INDIGO.

Claſs 17. Order 3. Diadelphia Decandria.

THE *Empalement* is of one leaf, tubulous, cylindrical and top-ſhaped: at the mouth erect, five-toothed, and obtuſe: the two ſuperior teeth largeſt; permanent.

The *Corolla* is a ſingle petal, inverſe egg-ſhape, concave, ſcarce larger than the calyx, erect, inſerted in the calyx between the two largeſt upper teeth, and placed on the upper ſide.

The

The *Filaments* are ten, very ſlightly joined at the baſe, erect, unequal in length, and longer than the corolla. The *Antheræ* are ſimple.

The *Germen* is roundiſh. The *Style* awl-ſhaped and the length of the *Stamina*. The *Stigma* is ſimple.

The *Seed-veſſel* a Legumen or Pod, moon-ſhaped, reflexed, larger than the calyx, compreſſed, the top moſt reflexed, of one cell, and tubercled.

The *Seeds* are two, of an oblong kidney form.

Obſ. This is ſingularly diſtinguiſhable from all the Papilionaceous tribe, in having only the vexillum or ſtandard, and wanting the wings and keel.

There appears to be but one Species *of this Genus*, viz.

AMORPHA fruticoſa. *Shrubby Baſtard Indigo.*

This grows naturally in Carolina, where it riſes with many irregular ſtems, to the height of ten or twelve feet, with very long winged leaves, in ſhape like thoſe of the common Acacia. At the extremity of the ſame year's ſhoots, the flowers are produced in long ſlender ſpikes, which are very ſmall and of a deep purple colour. The flowers are ſucceeded by moon-ſhaped, reflexed, compreſſed pods, each containing two kidney-ſhaped ſeeds.

ANDROMEDA.

ANDROMEDA.

Claſs 10. Order 1. Decandria Monogynia.

THE *Empalement* is five-parted, acute, very ſmall, coloured, and permanent.

The *Corolla* conſiſts of one petal, bell-ſhaped and five-cleft: the diviſions reflexed.

The *Filaments* are ten, awl-ſhaped, longer than and ſcarcely affixed to the corolla. The *Antheræ* are two horned and nodding.

The *Germen* is roundiſh. The *Style* cylindrical, longer than the Stamina and permanent. The *Stigma* is obtuſe.

The *Seed-veſſel* a capſule, roundiſh, pentagonal, five-celled, five valved, and gaping at the angles.

The

The *Seeds* are many, roundiſh and ſhining.

Obſ. The Corolla in ſome is ovate, in others perfectly bell-ſhaped.

The Species *are, native with us,*

1. ANDROMEDA arborea. *The Sorrel Tree.*

It grows naturally in Virginia, to about ten or twelve feet high. The flowers grow in long naked bunches, coming out from the ſides of the branches, of an herbaceous colour, ranged on one ſide of the common foot-ſtalk: they are oval, pitcher-ſhaped, and nodding; and are ſucceeded by ſmall capſules.

2. ANDROMEDA calyculata. *Ever-green Dwarf Andromeda.*

This is a low ſhrub, growing on moſſy land. The leaves are ſhaped ſomething like thoſe of the Box tree, and are of the ſame conſiſtence, having many ſmall punctures on them. The flowers grow in ſhort racemi or bunches from the extremity of the branches, they are white and of a cylindrical pitcher-ſhape.

3. ANDROMEDA paniculata. *Panicled Andromeda.*

This ſhrub grows in boggy wet ground, riſing from two or three to ſix or ſeven feet high, ſending out ſeveral branches which are clothed with oblong leaves, a little notched and placed alternately. The flowers grow in long looſe panicled *racemi* or bunches, at the extremity of the branches; they are pitcher-ſhaped, and ſucceeded by ſmall round ſeed-veſſels, having five cells, filled with ſmall round ſeeds. There is a variety of this of low growth, differing in having ſhorter

ſhorter panicled bunches of flowers, and theſe coming out at the diviſions, as well as at the extremities of the branches.

4. ANDROMEDA racemoſa. *Pennſylvanian Red-bud Andromeda.*

This grows in low clayed lands, to the height of five or ſix feet. The leaves are oblong and ſerrated. The flowers are produced in a one ſided *racemus* at the extremity of the branches, and reſemble the other kinds. The long bunch of flower buds are of a beautiful red colour in the ſpring, and thereby make a good appearance.

5. ANDROMEDA mariana. *Maryland, or broad-leaved Andromeda.*

Is a ſhrub of low growth, having but a ſmall ſtem, which is generally retroflected or bent from ſide to ſide. The leaves are egg-ſhaped, entire, broad, and of pretty thick conſiſtence. The Seed-veſſels are larger than the other kinds, gaping at their tops.

6. ANDROMEDA nitida. *Ever-green ſhining-leaved Andromeda, or Carolinian Red-buds.*

(Bartram's Catalogue.)

This ſhrub grows naturally in Carolina and Florida, and may juſtly be ranked among the moſt beautiful flowering.

The leaves are perennial, near three inches in length and one in breadth, of a hard and firm texture, lance-ſhape, of a deep ſhining, or gloſſy green colour on both ſides, placed by pretty long footſtalks alternately upon each ſide of the branches, but inclining

clining to the upper ſide, and ſtanding nearly erect. The flowers are produced along the under ſide of the branches, in long one rowed *racemi* or bunches, which as they arrive to their full growth change to a damaſk roſe colour. The under parts of the bunches ſomewhat reſemble the cells of a honey-comb, diffuſing an agreeable fragrance, and affording a delicious harveſt to the honey-bee.

7. ANDROMEDA plumata. *Plumed Andromeda, or Carolinian Iron-wood Tree.*

(Bartram's Catalogue.)

This is alſo a ſouthern beautiful ſpecies of Andromeda; riſing to the height of fifteen or twenty feet, and ſending off towards the top, many ſpreading and nearly horizontal branches.

The leaves are ſmall, lance-ſhaped, and of a deep gloſſy green, but changing in Autumn before they fall off, to yellow, red, purple, &c. giving the trees a beautiful appearance, even in their decline. The flowers are produced at the extremity of the branches, in one-rowed racemes or bunches, they are very ſmall and perfectly white, ſomewhat reſembling a plume of delicate white feathers. This and the laſt mentioned, grow naturally by the ſides of ponds, and ſwamps, in Carolina and Florida.

A N N O N A.

PAPAW TREE, or CUSTARD APPLE.

Claſs 13. Order 7. Polyandria Polygynia.

THE *Empalement* is three leaved and ſmall: the leaves heart-ſhaped, concave, and ſharp-pointed.

The *Corolla* is compoſed of ſix petals, heart-ſhaped and ſeſſile or ſquat: the three alternate interior leſs.

The *Filaments* ſcarce any. The *Antheræ* are very numerous, ſitting upon the ſides of the Germen.

The *Germen* is ſomewhat round, ſitting upon a roundiſh receptacle. The *Styles* none. The *Stigmas* obtuſe.

The *Seed-veſſel* a very large berry or fruit, of an oval or oblong ſhape, covered with a ſmooth rind, and of one cell.

The *Seeds* are ſeveral, hard, ſhining, oblong, oval, (compreſſed in ſome ſpecies) and placed in a circle.

The Species *with us are,*

1. ANNONA glabra. *Carolinian Smooth-barked Annona.*

The bark is ſmooth, the leaves broad, oval, but narrowed towards the baſe. The fruit is large, yellow and ſomewhat conical. This grows naturally in Carolina.

2. ANNONA triloba. *Pennſylvanian Triple-fruited Papaw.*

This grows common in rich bottoms and by river ſides, in Pennſylvania. It riſes to the height of ten, twelve, and ſometimes twenty feet, with but few branches, garniſhed with pretty long large leaves, narrowed toward the baſe and ſmooth on their edges. The flowers are ſolitary, and of a dark purple colour; they have ſhort footſtalks, which with the flower-cup is covered with ſhort brown hairs or down. The fruit is often found growing two or three together, which ſoon falls off, becomes very mellow and turns of a yellow colour.

ARALIA.

THE ANGELICA TREE.

Claſs 5. Order 5. Pentandria Pentagyina.

AN *Involucrum*, which is very ſmall, to the little globular umbels.

The

The *Empalement* is five-toothed, very ſmall, and above.

The *Corolla* conſiſts of five petals, which are ovate, acute, ſeſſile and reflexed.

The *Filaments* are five, awl-ſhaped, and the length of the corolla. The *Antheræ* are roundiſh.

The *Germen* is roundiſh and beneath. The *Styles* five, very ſhort, and permanent. The *Stigmas* ſimple.

The *Seed-veſſel* a berry, roundiſh, ſtriated, crowned and five-celled.

The *Seeds* are ſolitary, hard, and oblong.

The Species *with us are,*

ARALIA ſpinoſa. *Virginian Angelica Tree.*

This riſes with a thick woody ſtem to the height of ten or twelve feet, dividing into ſeveral branches, which are garniſhed with ramoſe divaricated leaves, placed alternately. The flowers are produced in large, looſe, compound umbels, at the extremity of the branches: they are of an herbaceous colour, and are ſucceeded by roundiſh berries of a purpliſh colour when ripe. The ſtem, branches, and footſtalks of the leaves are armed with ſhort ſtrong ſpines.

ARBUTUS.

THE STRAWBERRY TREE, OR BEAR-BERRY.

Claſs 10. Order 1. Decandria Monogynia.

THE *Empalement* is five parted, obtuſe, very ſmall and permanent.

The *Corolla* is one petalled, ovate, planiſh at the baſe; the border is five cleſt; the diviſions obtuſe, revolute and ſmall.

The *Filaments* are ten, awl-bellied, very ſlender at the baſe, half the length of the corolla, and affixed by the margin to its baſe. The *Antheræ* are ſlightly two cleſt and nodding.

The *Germen* is ſomewhat globoſe, ſitting upon a receptacle marked with ten points. The *Style* is cylindrical and the length of the corolla. The *Stigma* is thickiſh and obtuſe.

The *Seed-veſſel* is a berry, roundiſh and five celled.

The *Seeds* are ſmall and bony.

The

The Species *with us are,*

ARBUTUS Uva urſi. *The Bear-berry.*

This grows naturally in the Jerſeys. It is a low trailing ſhrub, dividing into many branches, cloſely ſet with ſmooth, thick, entire leaves, of an oval form. The flowers are produced in ſmall bunches, near the ends of the branches, and are ſucceeded by red berries. This has been uſed with great ſucceſs in many calculous complaints.

ARISTOLOCHIA.

BIRTHWORT.

Claſs 20. Order 5. Gynandria Hexagynia.

THE *Empalement* is wanting.

The *Corolla* is of one petal, tubulous and irregular: the *baſe* bellied, ſomewhat globular and protuberant: the *tube* oblong, ſix cornered cylindrical: the *border* dilated and extended beneath in a long tongue.

The *Filaments* are wanting. The *Antheræ* are ſix adjoined under the *Stigmas*, and four celled.

The *Germen* is oblong beneath and angled. The *Style* ſcarce any. The *Stigma* ſomewhat globular, ſix parted, and concave.

The *Seed-veſſel* is a capſule, which is large, hexagonal and ſix celled.

The *Seeds* are many, depreſſed and incumbent.

Obſ. The *Seed-veſſel* varies in figure; in ſome ſpecies it is roundiſh, in others oblong.

The Species *growing ſhrubby, with us, is one,* viz.

ARISTOLOCHIA fruteſcens. *Pennſylvanian Shrubby Birthwort.*

This grows naturally near Pittſburg, in a rich ſoil and ſhaded ſituation; riſing with ſhrubby cylindri-

cal

cal ſtems, which twine round any neighbouring ſupport, and reach ſometimes to the height of thirty feet or more, ſending off many long twining branches. The leaves are large, entire, and heart-ſhaped, of eight inches or more in length, and as much in breadth, ſtanding upon thick ſtrong foot-ſtalks. The flowers come out ſingly, or ſometimes two together upon pretty long foot-ſtalks, which are either terminal, or ariſe beneath the diviſions of the branches, each having a bractea or floral leaf embracing it near its baſe; they conſiſt of a long tube which is very crooked and bellied towards the baſe, but narrower towards the extremity, and furniſhed with a border which at firſt appears three lobed and triangular (in form of a cock'd hat,) but after becomes ſpreading, plain and roundiſh, and together with the interior extremity of the tube, is finely variegated with ſpots or ſtreaks. The Capſules or Seed-veſſels are cylindrical ſix-ſided, of three or four inches in length and near one in diameter, opening with ſix fiſſures, and having ſix cells, filled with heart-ſhaped compreſſed ſeeds, with a falſe one between each. This from its twining ſtems and large leaves affords a fine ſhady covering for an arbour.

The roots have an aromatic penetrating ſavour, and are ſuppoſed to be equal in medical virtues to the ſmall Virginian Snake-root.

A S C Y R U M.

St. P E T E R's W O R T.

Claſs 18. Order 3. Polyadelphia Polyandria.

THE *Empalement* is of four leaves; the exterior oppoſite are very ſmall and linear; the interior heart-ſhaped, plane, large, and erect, and all permanent.

The

The *Corolla* is of four petals, ovate: the exterior opposite largest, the interior less.

The *Filaments* are numerous, bristly, slightly joined at the base into four parts. The *Antheræ* are roundish.

The *Germen* is oblong. The *Style* scarce any. The *Stigma* simple.

The *Seed-vessel* a Capsule, oblong, sharp pointed, and enclosed by the larger leaves of the empalement.

The *Seeds* are numerous, small and roundish.

The Species *are*,

1. ASCYRUM Hypericoides. *St. Peter's Wort.*

This is a small shrubby plant, growing naturally in low moist ground, and rising with a few slender stems to the height of about eighteen inches, having small opposite branches, which are somewhat flatted. The leaves are small, oblong, somewhat wedge-shape, placed opposite, and sitting close. The flowers are sparingly produced at the tops of the stalks, and have somewhat the appearance of those of St. John's wort.

2. ASCYRUM villosum. *Villose St. Peter's wort.*

This rises to the height of about three feet, with erect stalks. The leaves are oblong and hairy. The flowers are produced at the tops of the stalks, resembling those of St. John's wort, but have only four petals.

AZALEA.

UPRIGHT HONEY-SUCKLE.

Class 5. Order 1. Pentandria Monogynia.

THE *Empalement* is five parted, erect, acute, small, coloured and permanent.

The

The *Corolla* is monopetalous, bell-ſhaped, and half five-cleft: the ſide diviſions inflexed.

The *Filaments* are five, filiform, free, unequal in length, and inſerted in the receptacle. The *Antheræ* are ſimple.

The *Germen* is roundiſh. The *Style* filiform, the length of the corolla and permanent. The *Stigma* is obtuſe.

The *Seed-veſſel* is a Capſule, roundiſh, five cell'd, and five valv'd.

The *Seeds* are ſeveral, roundiſh.

Obſ. The figure of the petal in ſome Species is funnel form, in others bell-ſhaped; the ſtamina in ſome are alſo very long and declined.

The Species *with us, are,*

1. AZALEA nudiflora. *Red-flowered Azalea.*

This grows moſt common upon a moiſt, clayey, gravelly ſoil, riſing from two or three, to five or ſix feet in height. The leaves are produced in cluſters at the extremity of the branches; they are oblong, inverſe, egg-ſhaped, and a little hairy upon their edges and midribs underneath. The flowers are produced early in the ſpring before the leaves are expanded, in heads or cluſters at the ends of the ſtalks and chief branches, of a red colour, and hairy, with very long red ſtamina. There is great variety in the colour of the flowers, from red to almoſt white.

2. AZALEA viſcoſa. *White ſweet Azalea.*

This grows naturally in rich rocky places, near ſtreams of water; riſing to the height of five or ſix feet. The leaves are much ſmaller and of a paler green colour than thoſe of the red flowered, otherwiſe reſembling them. The flowers are produced after the leaves are fully expanded, (about harveſt time;) they are white, hairy and clammy, and have the fragrance of the honey-ſuckle.

3. Azalea viſcoſa paluſtris. *Swamp Azalea.*

This is a variety of the white kind, growing naturally in wet low ground. It is of lower growth, with leaves rough and clammy at their firſt appearance. The flowers are white, but not ſo ſweet as the former. There is alſo ſome other varieties differing ſomewhat in the diſpoſition or appearance of their flowers, &c.

BACCHARIS.

PLOWMAN's SPIKENARD.

Claſs 19. Order 2. Syngeneſia Polygamia Superflua.

THE *Common Calyx* is cylindrical, and imbricated: the *Scales* linear and acute.

The *Compound Corolla*, is equal with *Florets* Hermaphrodite and Female mixed.

The *Proper* of the hermaphrodite is funnel-form and five cleft.
——— of the female ſcarce manifeſt, or almoſt none.

The *Filaments* of the *hermaphrodite* are five, capillary and very ſmall. The *Antheræ* cylindrical and tubulous.

The *Germen* of the hermaphrodite is ovate. The *Style* filiform and the length of the flower. The *Stigma* is bifid or two cleft.

Of the *female* very like the hermaphrodite.

The *Seed-veſſel* none, but the calyx changed.

The *Seeds* of the hermaphrodite and female much alike, ſolitary, very ſhort, and oblong. The *Pappus* ſimple.

The *Receptacle* is naked.

The Species *are*,

Baccharis halimifolia. *Virginian Groundſel Tree.*

It riſes to the height of ſix or eight feet, ſending out many erect branches, garniſhed with leaves which

which are ſomewhat ovate, and a little toothed above, continuing green moſt of the year. The flowers are produced at the extremity of the branches, and are of a yellowiſh white colour.

BERBERIS.

The BARBERRY-BUSH.

Claſs 6. Order 1. Hexandria Monogynia.

THE *Empalement* is ſix leaved and ſpreading; the leaves ovate, narrower at the baſe; concave, the alternate leſs, coloured, and deciduous.

The *Corolla* is of ſix petals, which are roundiſh, concave, ſomewhat ſpreading, and ſcarce larger than the calyx.

A *Nectarium* of two corpuſles, roundiſh, coloured and affixed to the baſe of each petal.

The *Filaments* are ſix, erect, compreſſed and obtuſe. Two *Antheræ* are joined to the top of each filament.

The *Germen* is cylindrical and the length of the ſtamina. The *Style* is wanting. The *Stigma* is orbiculate, broader than the germen, and ſurrounded by an acute margin.

The *Seed-veſſel* is a berry, which is cylindrical, obtuſe and of one cell.

The *Seeds* are two, oblong, cylindrical and obtuſe.

The Species *are,*

BERBERIS canadienſis. *The Canadian Barberry.*

This grows naturally in Canada, and ſomewhat reſembles the European Barberry, except the leaves being much ſhorter and broader, and the fruit, when ripe, of a black colour. There is alſo a kind of Barberry growing upon New-River in Virginia, bearing red berries, of which I have ſeen one ſmall plant.

BETULA.

The BIRCH-TREE.

Claſs 21. Order 4. Monoecia Tetrandria.

*THE *Male* flowers are diſpoſed in a cylindrical Katkin.

The *Calyx*, is a common Katkin, imbricated on all ſides, looſe and cylindrical; compoſed of triflorous *Scales*, to each of which, two very minute ſcales are placed at the ſides.

The *Compound Corolla* conſiſts of three florets, equal, and affixed to the diſk of each ſcale of the Katkin.

The *Proper* is monopetalous, four-parted, ſpreading, and ſmall: the diviſions obtuſe and egg-ſhaped.

The *Filaments* are four, very ſmall. The *Antheræ* are twin.

*The *Female* flowers are diſpoſed in Katkins on the ſame plant.

The *Calyx* is a common Katkin, imbricated: with three ſcales every where oppoſed, affixed to the *rachis*, heart ſhaped with a point, biflorous, a little divided by a pointed body in the boſom towards the top, concave, and ſhort.

The *Corolla* none manifeſt.

The *Germen* proper, is ovate, very ſmall. The *Styles* are two, briſtly, and the length of the ſcales. The *Stigmas* ſimple.

The *Seed-veſſel* none. The Katkin embracing the ſeeds of two florets under each ſcale.

The *Seeds* are ſolitary and ovate.

The Species *with us are,*

1. BETULA nigra. *Black, or Sweet-Birch.*

This becomes a large tree, often riſing to the height of fifty or ſixty feet, and ſending off many branches. The leaves are egg-ſhaped and doubly or irregularly ſerrated, the ſmall ſerratures are cloſe, the larger more remote; their footſtalks are villoſe. The ſmall branches are alſo covered with down. The natives often make their canoes of the bark of this tree.

2. BETULA

2. BETULA lenta. *Red Birch.*

This grows to a pretty large ſize, ſpreading into many ſlender pliable branches. The leaves are ſmooth, heart-ſhaped, oblong, ſharp-pointed, and finely and ſlightly ſawed on their edges.

3. BETULA papyrifera. *White Paper Birch.*

This is a variety of the laſt, growing to a middling ſize and pretty much reſembling it, except in having a very white ſmooth bark.

4. BETULA populifolia. *Aſpen-leaved Birch.*

This is alſo a variety of the ſecond, and grows naturally in the Jerſeys, and other eaſtern ſtates, becoming a pretty tall tree, and covered with a white bark. The leaves are ſomewhat triangular, like thoſe of the Aſpen tree, but terminating in a long acute point; they are doubly ſerrated, ſtanding upon long ſlender footſtalks, and are put in motion by the ſlighteſt breeze of wind.

5. BETULA humilis. *Dwarf Birch.*

This is alſo a variety of the ſecond kind, of a low and dwarfiſh growth.

BETULA-ALNUS.

The ALDER TREE.

THE Characters are the ſame of the Betula, except the *Seed-veſſel* being a roundiſh cone.

The Species *are,*

1. BETULA

1. BETULA-ALNUS glauca. *Silver-leaved Alder.*

This grows naturally in low marſhy ground, and frequently riſes to the height of ten or twelve feet.

2. BETULA-ALNUS maritima. *Sea-ſide Alder.*

This grows to the height of the former. The leaves are long and narrow. The katkins are generally in bloom in Auguſt, at which time the female cone or ſeed-veſſel ſets, but don't grow to perfection till the next ſummer.

3. BETULA-ALNUS rubra. *Common Alder.*

This grows very common in moſt parts of Pennſylvania. The leaves are broader than the other kinds, and rough or wrinkled. This flowers in the ſpring, and perfects its ſeeds in the fall.

BIGNONIA.

The TRUMPET FLOWER.

Claſs 14. Order 1. Didynamia Angioſpermia.

THE *Empalement* is of one leaf, erect, cup-form, and five-cleft.

The *Corolla* is monopetalous, and bell-ſhaped. The tube very ſmall and the length of the calyx. The chaps very long, bellied underneath, and of an oblong bell-ſhape. The border is five parted; the two ſuperior diviſions reflexed; the inferior ſpreading.

The *Filaments* are four, awl-ſhaped and ſhorter than the corolla, of which two are longer than the reſt. The *Antheræ* are reflexed, oblong, and as if doubled.

The *Germen* is oblong. The *Style* thread-form, of the ſituation and ſhape of the ſtamina. The *Stigma* is headed.

The

The *Seed-veſſel* is a ſiliqua or pod, of two cells and two valves.
The *Seeds* are pretty many, imbricated, compreſſed, and having a membranaceous wing.

Obſ. The Catalpa delights in only two perfect ſtamina, and three imperfect rudiments, with a pentaphyllous calyx.

The Species *are,*

1. BIGNONIA Catalpa. *The Catalpa-Tree.*

This riſes to the height of twelve or fifteen feet, with a ſtrong ſtem, dividing into ſeveral branches, which are garniſhed with large heart-ſhaped leaves, placed oppoſite at each joint. The flowers are produced in large branching panicles, at the ends of the branches; of a dirty white colour, with a few purple ſpots, and faint ſtripes of yellow on the inſide; and waved on their edges: they are ſucceeded by very long ſlender pods, filled with flat winged ſeeds, lying over each other like the ſcales of a fiſh.

2. BIGNONIA crucigera. *Croſs-vine.*

This riſes with ſlender trailing ſtalks, which muſt be ſupported, ſo require the aſſiſtance of a wall, and a good aſpect; being impatient of much cold. The branches are clothed with oblong leaves remaining green all the year. The flowers are produced at the wings of the leaves, ſhaped much like thoſe of the Fox-glove; and are of a yellow colour.

3. BIGNONIA radicans. *Climing Trumpet-Flower.*

This kind, when old, hath large rough ſtems, which ſend out many trailing branches, putting out roots at their joints, thereby attaching themſelves to any neighbouring ſupport, and riſing ſometimes to the

the height of forty or fifty feet. The branches are garniſhed with winged leaves placed oppoſite, which are generally compoſed of four pair of ſmall leaves, terminated by an odd one. The flowers are produced at the ends of the ſhoots of the ſame year, in large bunches; they have long ſwelling tubes, ſhaped ſomewhat like a trumpet, and are of an orange colour, inclining to red; and ſucceeded by large pods full of winged ſeeds.

4. BIGNONIA ſempervirens. *Ever-green Bignonia, or Yellow Jaſmine.*

This kind reſembles the ſecond ſo much as to require no further deſcription.

CALLICARPA.

CALLICARPA.

Claſs 4. Order 1. Tetrandria Monogynia.

THE *Empalement* is of one leaf, bell-ſhaped: at the mouth four-parted and erect.

The *Corolla* is of one petal, tubulous: The border four-cleſt, obtuſe and ſpreading.

The *Filaments* are four, thread-form, twice the length of the corolla. The *Antheræ* ovate and incumbent.

The *Germen* is roundiſh. The *Style* thread form, thicker above. The *Stigma* thickiſh and obtuſe.

The *Seed-veſſel* is a berry, globoſe and ſmooth.

The *Seeds* are four, ſmall, callous, oval, compreſſed, ſomewhat convex on one ſide, but a little hallowed as if eaten on the other.

There is but one Species *of this Genus*, viz.

CALLICARPA americana. *Carolinian Shrubby Callicarpa.*

This ſhrub riſes from three to five feet high, with but ſlender ſtems, ſending out many branches from the

the ſides, which are wooly or downy when young, garniſhed with oval, ſpear-ſhaped leaves, placed oppoſite on pretty long footſtalks. The flowers come out in whorls round the ſtalks, ſitting very cloſe; they are ſmall and tubulous, cut into four obtuſe ſegments at the top, which expand and are of a deep purple colour; theſe are ſucceeded by ſoft ſucculent berries, which are of a deep purple colour when full ripe, each encloſing four hard ſeeds. This is a native of Carolina and will not endure much cold.

CALYCANTHUS.

CAROLINIAN ALLSPICE.

Claſs 12. Order 5. Icoſandria Polygynia.

THE *Calyx* is of one leaf, thickened, ſquarroſe, ſomewhat top-ſhaped, truncated, almoſt cloſed above; and permanent.

The *Corolla* is compoſed of many leaves, which are oblong, coloured, of thick and fleſhy conſiſtence, longer than the calyx, ſomewhat ſpreading, but chiefly lightly incurved their whole length; inſerted in the truncated margin of the calyx, diſpoſed in ſeveral ſeries or rows circularly, of unequal length and deciduous.

The *Filaments* are many, ſhort, awl-ſhaped and inſerted in the top of the calyx; the exterior of which, have oblong furrowed *Antheræ* adjoined to their apex; the interior barren and cloſing the calyx.

The *Germen* are many, oblong, villoſe, and hid within the calyx.

The *Styles* many, joined in a medullary column and protruding in the center of the barren filaments, which ſerve for its defence.

The *Seed-veſſel* none but the calyx, thickened, much enlarged, berry'd, and ſomewhat inverſe egg-ſhaped.

The *Seeds* are many, oval, ſomewhat villoſe, and ſurrounded longitudinally with a ſuture.

We have but one Species *of this Genus,* viz.

CALYCANTHUS

CALYCANTHUS floridus. *Carolinian Allſpice.*

This delightful ſweet-ſcented ſhrub, grows naturally in Carolina, and riſes from four to ſix or eight feet high, ſending out many ſmall branches, which are placed oppoſite and garniſhed with oval entire leaves; which are likewiſe oppoſite. The flowers are produced ſingly, at the extremities of the ſame year's ſhoots; they are of a ſullen or dark purple colour, and when ſomewhat expanded, diffuſe to a conſiderable diſtance, a very agreeable ſcent, ſcarcely diſtinguiſhable from that of ripe ſtrawberries. It flowers in May, and by ſucceſſion till almoſt harveſt. The flowers are ſucceeded by large, ſomewhat oval, rough, ſwelling capſules, of two inches or more in length, and one in diameter, containing many oval brown ſeeds.

CARPINUS.

The HORNBEAM-TREE.

Claſs 21. Order 8. Monoecia Polyandria.

* THE *Male Flowers* are diſpoſed in a cylindrical Katkin.
The *Calyx* is a common Katkin looſely imbricated on all ſides: compoſed of ſcales which are uniflorous, ovate, concave, acute, and ciliated.
The *Corolla* is none.
The *Filaments* are for the moſt part ten, very ſmall. The *Antheræ* are twin, compreſſed, villoſe at the apex, and two valved.
* The *Female Flowers* are diſpoſed in a long Katkin, on the ſame plant.
The *Calyx* is a common Katkin looſely imbricated, conſiſting of *Scales* which are lance-ſhaped, villoſe, reflexed at the apex, and one flowered.
The *Corolla* is cup-form, of one leaf, ſix cleft, with two diviſions larger.

The

The *Germen* are two, very ſhort, each having two *Styles*, which are long, capillary and coloured. The *Stigmas* are ſimple.
The *Seed-veſſel* none. The Katkin being enlarged and containing a ſeed at the baſe of each ſcale.
The *Seed* is a nut, ovate and angled.

Obſ. The ſeeds of the Carpinus Betulus are contained within the baſe of the concave calycine ſcale: but of the Oſtrya within the inflated ſcale.

The Species *are, with us,*

1. CARPINUS Betulus virginiana. *American Hornbeam.*

This grows common by moſt of our river and creek ſides, riſing with a ſtrong, woody, ſomewhat angular ſtem, to the height of ten or fifteen feet; ſpreading into many branches, with oval, pointed leaves, ſawed on their edges. The flowers are produced at the ends of the young ſhoots, in looſe, leaffy katkins, and are ſucceeded by ſmall, hard, angular ſeeds.

2. CARPINUS Oſtrya. *The Hop-Hornbeam.*

This tree often grows larger and more upright than the former, the wood is tougher, the branches fewer and more erect. The leaves ſomewhat reſemble thoſe of the Elm. The male katkins are produced at the extremity of the branches, they are ſet the preceding fall, and remain all winter. The female flowers are produced in inflated chaffy katkins, much reſembling a hop, from whence it acquired its name. There is a variety of this called the *Virginian flowering* Hop-Hornbeam, which I have not ſeen.

CASSINE.

CASSINE.

CASSINE, or SOUTH-SEA TEA-TREE.

Claſs 5. Order 3. Pentandria Trigynia.

THE *Empalement* is five-parted, beneath, very ſmall, obtuſe, and permanent.

The *Corolla* is five-parted and ſpreading; the diviſions are ſomewhat ovate, obtuſe, and larger than the calyx.

The *Filaments* are five, awl-ſhaped and ſpreading. The *Antheræ* are ſimple.

The *Germen* is above and conical. The *Style* none. The *Stigmas* three, reflexed and obtuſe.

The *Seed-veſſel* is a berry, roundiſh, three-cell'd and umbilicated with the Stigmas.

The *Seeds* are ſolitary and ſomewhat ovate.

The Species *are*,

CASSINE Paragua. *Ever-green Caſſine, Yapon, or South-Sea Tea-tree.*

This grows naturally in Carolina and ſome parts of Virginia, but chiefly near the ſea; and riſes to the height of ten or twelve feet, ſending out branches from the ground upward, garniſhed with Ever-green ſpear-ſhaped leaves, placed alternately: they are of a deep green colour, of a thick conſiſtence and a little notched on their edges. The flowers are produced in cloſe whorls, round the branches, at the footſtalks of the leaves; they are white, and are ſucceeded by red berries, with three cells, each containing a ſingle ſeed.

CEANOTHUS.

CEANOTHUS.

The NEW-JERSEY TEA-TREE.

Claſs 5. Order 1. Pentandria Monogynia.

THE *Empalement* is of one leaf, top-ſhaped: the border is five-parted, acute, and incurved; and permanent.

The *Corolla* is compoſed of five petals, equal, roundiſh, hook-ſacked, compreſſed, very obtuſe, ſpreading, leſs than the calyx, with claws the length of the petal, riſing from the inciſions of the calyx.

The *Filaments* are five, awl-ſhaped, erect, oppoſite to the petals, and longer than the corolla. The *Antheræ* are roundiſh.

The *Germen* is three cornered. The *Style* is cylindrical, half three-cleft, and the length of the Stamina. The *Stigma* obtuſe.

The *Seed-veſſel* is a berry, which is dry, three fruited, three-cell'd, obtuſe, and ſet with tubercles.

The *Seeds* are ſolitary and ovate.

The Species *with us, but one,* viz.

CEANOTHUS americanus. *American Ceanothus, or New-Jerſey Tea-tree.*

This is a low ſhrub, growing common in moſt parts of North America; ſeldom riſing above four or five feet high, and ſending out branches on every ſide from the ground upward, which are garniſhed with oval, pointed leaves, having three longitudinal veins, running from the foot-ſtalk to the point, diverging from each other in the middle; they are placed oppoſite, and are of a light green colour. The flowers are produced at the extremity of the ſhoots, in a cloſe kind of *Thyrſus;* they are of a white colour and when in bloom make a fine appearance. A decoction of the roots of this ſhrub is eſteemed a certain cure, not only in ſlight Gonor-

rhæa's,

rhæa's, which it ſtops in two or three days, without any bad conſequences; but alſo in the moſt inveterate Venereal complaints. The leaves are dried and uſed by ſome as a ſubſtitute for Bohea Tea, from which it acquired its name.

CELASTRUS.

The STAFF-TREE.

Claſs 5. Order 1. Pentandria Monogynia.

THE *Empalement* is of one leaf, half-five-cleft, plane, and very ſmall: the diviſions are obtuſe and unequal.

The *Corolla* has five petals, ovate, ſpreading, ſeſſile, equal and reflexed at their margins.

The *Filaments* are five, awl-ſhaped and the length of the corolla. The *Antheræ* are very ſmall.

The *Germen* is very ſmall, immerſed in the receptacle, which is large, plane, and marked with ten ſtreaks. The *Style* is awl-ſhaped and ſhorter than the ſtamina. The *Stigma* is obtuſe, and three-cleft.

The *Seed-veſſel* is a Capſule, coloured, ovate, obtuſely three-cornered, gibbous, three cell'd, and three valv'd.

The *Seeds* are few, ovate, coloured, ſmooth, and half covered with an Arillus, four parted at the mouth, unequal and coloured.

The Species *but one, with us,* viz.

CELASTRUS ſcandens. *American Climing Staff-tree.*

This grows naturally in many parts of North-America, riſing with a twining woody ſtem to the height of ten or fifteen feet when ſupported, ſending out many ſlender flexible branches, cloathed with oblong pointed leaves, a little ſawed on their edges. The flowers come out from the ſides of the branches in looſe bunches; they are of an herbace-

ous

ous colour, and are ſucceeded by roundiſh three-cornered capſules, of a pale, or yellowiſh red colour when ripe; which ſpread open in three parts, diſcloſing their ſeeds after the manner of the Spindle Tree. The ſeeds are hard, oval and covered with a thin red pulp. It makes a very fine appearance when covered with ripe fruit.

CELTIS.

The NETTLE-TREE.

Claſs 23. Order 1. Polygamia Monoecia.

*THE *Hermaprodite* flowers are ſolitary and ſuperior.
The *Empalement* is one-leafed, and five-parted; the diviſions ovate, ſpreading and withering.
The *Corolla* is wanting.
The *Filaments* are five, very ſhort, hid by the Antheræ, but after the diſcharge of the farina, longer. The *Antheræ* are oblong, thickiſh, quadrangular, and four-furrowed.
The *Germen* is ovate, ſharp-pointed, and the length of calyx. The *Styles* are two, ſpreading, variouſly inflexed, awl-ſhaped, very long, and downy on all ſides. The *Stigmas* are ſimple.
The *Seed-veſſel* is a drupe, roundiſh and of one cell.
The *Seed* is a nut, which is roundiſh.
* The *Male* flowers are in the ſame plant, and inferior.
The *Empalement* is ſix-parted, otherwiſe as the *Hermaphrodite.*
The *Corolla* is wanting.
The *Filaments* are as in the *Hermaphrodite.*

The Species *with us, but one,* viz.

CELTIS occidentalis. *American Yellow-fruited Nettle-tree.*

This grows naturally in many parts of North-America. It delights in a rich, moiſt ſoil, in which it becomes a large tree, riſing with a ſtraight ſtem, the bark of which, in young trees, is ſometimes ſmooth

ſmooth and of a dark colour, but as they advance becomes rougher and of a lighter colour. The branches are ſet thick on every ſide, and garniſhed with oblique oval leaves, ending in points and ſawed on their edges. The flowers come out oppoſite to the leaves, upon pretty long footſtalks; they are ſmall and make but little appearance, and are ſucceeded by round, hard berries, about the ſize of a ſmall pea, of a yellow colour and ſweet taſte when ripe. The juice of the fruit is ſaid to be aſtringent and to give eaſe in violent Dyſenteries.

CEPHALANTHUS.

The BUTTON-TREE.

Claſs 4. Order 1. Tetrandria Monogynia.

THE *Common Empalement* is none, but a globoſe receptacle, collecting many florets into a little head.

The *Proper Empalement* is one leaved, funnel-form and angular; the border four-cleft.

The *Univerſal Corolla* is equal. The *Proper* of one petal, funnel-form and acute.

The *Filaments* are four, inſerted in the corolla, and ſhorter than the border. The *Antheræ* are globoſe.

The *Germen* is beneath. The *Style* longer than the corolla. The *Stigma* globoſe.

The *Seedveſſel* none.

The *Seeds* are ſolitary, long, leſſened at the baſe, pyramidal and wooly.

The *Common Receptacle* is round and villoſe.

The Species *but one*, viz.

CEPHALANTHUS occidentalis. *Button-tree.*

This ſhrub grows pretty common by creek ſides and ponds, riſing to the height of ſix or eight feet; growing very crooked, and ſending out ſeveral branches,

branches, which grow oppoſite. The leaves are alſo placed oppoſite and often, upon young ſhoots, by three's; they are near three inches long and one and a quarter broad, having a ſtrong vein running longitudinally through them, they are of a light green and their footſtalks change to a reddiſh colour next the branches. The branches are terminated with globular heads, compoſed of many ſmall flowers, of a whitiſh colour.

CERCIS.

The JUDAS TREE.

Claſs 10. Order 1. Decandria Monogynia.

THE *Empalement* is of one leaf, very ſhort, bell-ſhaped, gibbous beneath, and melliferous: the mouth is five toothed, erect and obtuſe.

The *Corolla* is ten petal'd, inſerted in the calyx, and counterfeiting a papilionaceous corolla.

The *Wings*, are two petals, bent back, and affixed by long claws.

The *Standard*, one petal, roundiſh, clawed, under and ſhorter than the wings.

The *Keel*, two petals, joining in a heart-ſhaped figure, including the parts of fructification and affixed by claws.

The *Nectarium*, a gland, ſtyle form, under the germen.

The *Filaments* are ten, diſtinct, awl-ſhaped, declined, of which four are longer; and covered. The *Antheræ* are oblong, incumbent, and ariſing.

The *Germen* is linear-lanced and pedicel'd. The *Style* is of the length and ſituation of the ſtamina. The *Stigma* is obtuſe and ariſing.

The *Seed-veſſel* is a legumen or pod, which is oblong, acute, oblique pointed, and of one cell.

The *Seeds* are ſeveral, roundiſh and joined to the ſuperior ſuture.

The Species *with us, but one,* viz.

CERCIS

CERCIS canadenſis. *Red-bud, or Judas Tree.*

This grows naturally in ſeveral parts of North-America, riſing to the height of ten or fifteen feet, with a pretty ſtrong trunk covered with a darkiſh coloured bark; dividing upwards into ſeveral irregular branches, furniſhed with heart-ſhaped leaves, ſmooth upon their upper ſurface and edges, but a little downy underneath, having pretty long foot-ſtalks. The flowers come out upon the branches upon all ſides, many ariſing from the ſame point, with ſhort footſtalks; they are of a fine red colour and coming out before the leaves, make a beautiful appearance. There is ſaid to be a variety of this in Carolina, with ſmall flowers.

CHIONANTHUS.

The SNOW-DROP, or FRINGE TREE.

Claſs 2. Order 1. Diandria Monogynia.

THE *Empalement* is of one leaf, four-parted, erect, ſharp-pointed and permanent.

The *Corolla* is one petal'd and funnel-form. The *tube* is very ſhort, ſpreading, and the length of the caylx. The *border* with four diviſions, which are linear, erect, acute, oblique, and very long.

The *Filaments* are two, very ſhort, awl-ſhaped and inſerted in the tube. The *Antheræ* are heart-ſhaped, and erect.

The *Germen* is ovate. The *Style* ſimple and the length of the calyx. The *Stigma* is obtuſe and three-cleft.

The *ſeed-veſſel* is a drupe, roundiſh or oval and of one cell.

The *Seed* a ſtriated nut.

Obſ. The number of ſtamina is often three or four.

We have but one Species *in America*, viz.

CHIONANTHUS

CHIONANTHUS virginica. *Virginian Snow-drop Tree.*

This ſhrub grows naturally in ſeveral places in North America, in a moiſt ſoil; riſing to the height of fifteen or twenty feet, ſpreading into many branches, covered with a light coloured bark. The leaves are large, oblong and entire, placed nearly oppoſite. The flowers are produced towards the extremity of the ſhoots of the former year, upon ſhort, leaffy, common footſtalks; at the boſom of the leaves of which, the proper footſtalks come out, and are divided for the moſt part into three parts, but often more; each ſuſtaining one ſmall flower, with four very long, narrow, white petals; which, when fully grown, make a beautiful appearance: theſe are ſucceeded by oval berries, of a livid blackiſh colour when ripe, each containing one hard, oblong, pointed ſeed. The bark of the root of this ſhrub, bruiſed and applied to freſh wounds, is accounted by the natives a ſpecific, in healing them without ſuppuration.

CLETHRA.

CLETHRA.

Claſs 10. Order 1. Decandria Monogynia.

THE *Empalement* is of one leaf, five-parted; the leaves are ovate, concave, erect and permanent.

The *Corolla* conſiſts of five petals, oblong, broader without, a little ſpreading, and longer than the calyx.

The *Filaments* are ten, awl-ſhaped, and the length of the corolla. The *Antheræ* oblong-erect, gaping at the apex.

The *Germen* is roundiſh. The *Style* is thread-form, erect, permanent, and increaſing. The *Stigma* is three-cleft.

The *Seed-veſſel* is a capſule, roundiſh, covered with the calyx, three-cell'd and three-valv'd.

The *Seeds* are many and angled.

There is but one Species *of this Genus*, viz.

CLETHRA alnifolia. *Alder leaved Clethra.*

This ſhrub grows common in Maryland, Virginia, and Carolina, in moiſt ground and by rivulets; riſing to the height of ſix or eight feet, dividing into many branches, clothed with wedge-ſhape, oval, veined leaves, ſawed on their edges, reſembling thoſe of the Alder but longer; which are placed alternately. The flowers are produced at the extremity of the branches, in long cloſe bunches; they are of a white colour, and when in full bloom make a very fine appearance.

CORNUS.

The CORNEL, or DOGBERRY-TREE.

Claſs 4. Order 1. Tetrandria Monogynia.

THE *Calyx* conſiſts of an *Involucrum* of four leaves, many flowered: the leaves ovate, coloured, and deciduous; the oppoſite interior ſomewhat longer and narrower.

An *Empalement*, very ſmall, four-toothed, above and deciduous.

The *Corolla* conſiſts of four petals, oblong, acute, plane, and ſmaller than the Involucrum.

The *Filaments* are four, awl-ſhaped, erect, and longer than the corolla. The *Antheræ* are roundiſh and incumbent.

The *Germen* is roundiſh and beneath. The *Style* filiform and the length of the corolla. The *Stigma* is obtuſe.

The *Seed-veſſel* is a drupe, or ſtone-fruit, roundiſh and umbilicated.

The *Seed*, a nut, heart-ſhaped, or oblong, and two cell'd.

Obſ. The Involucrum is wanting in moſt of our Species.

The Species *are, with us,*

1. CORNUS

1. CORNUS alterna. *Alternate branched, or Female Virginian Dogwood.*

This grows to the height of twelve or fifteen feet, dividing upwards into many branches, which are covered with bark of a ſtriated or ſtreaked appearance. The ſmall branches are placed alternate, bending at each diviſion. The leaves are entire, oval, ſharp-pointed, and much veined. The flowers are produced in cluſters at the extremity of the branches, and are ſucceeded by roundiſh berries of a dark purple colour when ripe. The ſmall branches being alternate, afford a diſtinguiſhing mark for this ſpecies.

2. CORNUS candidiſſima. *Swamp American Dogwood.*

This ſhrub grows to the height of ſix or eight feet, moſtly in moiſt or ſwampy places; and is covered with a whitiſh bark. The branches are placed oppoſite, and alſo the leaves, which are lance-ſhaped and pointed, and of a whitiſh colour. The flowers are produced at the extremity of the branches, in cluſters, and are ſucceeded by whitiſh ſucculent berries.

3. CURNUS florida. *Male Virginian Dogwood.*

This riſes with a ſtrong ſtem to the height of twelve or fifteen feet, dividing into many ſpreading branches, which are ſometimes placed oppoſite, but often by four's, ariſing from oppoſite points and regularly diſpoſed. The leaves are oval, pointed, veined and entire. The flowers are produced at the extremity of the ſmall branches, in cluſters; having a common involucrum

involucrum of four large white leaves, which are generally end-bitten and a little coloured at their extremities, and one oppoſite pair, rather longer and narrower than the other. The flowers within are ſucceeded by oblong, red berries. This flowers in May and is deſervedly ranked amongſt the beautiful flowering ſhrubs. The bark of this kind has been uſed with ſome ſucceſs as a ſubſtitute for the Peruvian Bark. And to its top, regular diſpoſed ſhoots, our ſpinſters are often indebted for their diſtaffs.

4. CORNUS ſanguinea. *American Red-rod Cornus.*

This grows in a moiſt ſoil, to the height of eight or ten feet, generally many ſtems ariſing from the ſame root. The bark of the young ſhoots is very ſmooth, and of a beautiful dark red colour. The branches are placed oppoſite, and alſo the leaves, which much reſemble the firſt and third kinds above deſcribed. The flowers are produced in cluſters at the ends of the branches, of a whitiſh colour; and are ſucceeded by ſucculent berries of a bluiſh colour when ripe.

CORYLUS.

The HAZEL, or NUT-TREE.

Claſs 21, Order 8. Monoecia Polyandria.

*THE *Male* flowers are diſpoſed in a long Katkin.

The *Calyx*, a common Katkin, imbricated on all ſides, and cylindrical; conſiſting of *Scales*, which are uniflorous, narrowed at the baſe, at the apex broader, more obtuſe, inflexed and three-cleft: the middle diviſions of equal length, but twice the width of and covering the reſt.

The

The *Corolla* is wanting.

The *Filaments* are eight, very ſhort, joined to the interior ſide of the calycine ſcale. The *Antheræ* are oblong-ovate, ſhorter than the calyx, and erect.

* The *Female* flowers are remote from the *Male* in the ſame plant, ſitting cloſe and included in a bud.

The *Empalement* is of two leaves, coriaceous, torn at the margin, erect, and the length of the fruit; at the time of floreſcence, ſcarce manifeſt for its ſmallneſs.

The *Corolla* none.

The *Germen* is roundiſh and very ſmall. The *Styles* two, briſtly, coloured, and much longer than the calyx. The *Stigmas* are ſimple.

The *Seed-veſſel* none.

The *Seed*, a nut ſomewhat ovate, ſhaved at the baſe, ſomewhat compreſſed and pointed at the apex.

The Species *with us are,*

1. CORYLUS americana. *American Hazelnut.*

This grows very common in a rich, looſe, moiſt ſoil; ſpreading far by its roots, and riſing at firſt with a ſimple, erect ſtem; which, as it grows old, is divided into a few irregular branches, cloathed with oval, pointed leaves, ſawed on their edges. The Male katkins are produced at the ends of the branches, and the Female parts a little beneath them, often many together, at other times ſingly; and are ſucceeded by ſeed-veſſels, roundiſh at the baſe, but lengthened out into a leaffy, fringed expanſion, parted at the extremity; each containing one nut.

2. CORYLUS cornuta. *Dwarf Filbert, or Cuckold-nut.*

This kind much reſembles the other, except in ſize, ſeldom growing above three or four feet high; and alſo in having its nuts ſingle upon the branches, and

and their huſks or ſeed-veſſels ſmaller and lengthened out into a point or horn, and cloſely embracing its nuts.

CRATÆGUS.

The WILD SERVICE-TREE.

Claſs 12. Order 2. Icoſandria Digynia.

THE *Empalement* is one leaved, concave-ſpreading, five-toothed and permanent.

The *Corolla* is of five petals, roundiſh, concave, ſitting cloſe and inſerted in the calyx.

The *Filaments* are twenty, awl-ſhaped, and inſerted in the calyx. The *Antheræ* are roundiſh.

The *Germen* is beneath. The *Styles* are two, thread-form, and erect. The *Stigmas* are headed.

The *Seed-veſſel* is a berry, fleſhy, roundiſh, and umbilicated.

The *Seeds* are two, longiſh, diſtinct and cartilaginous.

Botanical writers enumerate ſeveral Species of this Genus, native of theſe ſtates; but I believe, upon more ſtrict examination, they will chiefly be found to belong, with more propriety, to the Meſpilus. *See* Meſpilus.

CUPRESSUS.

The CYPRESS TREE.

Claſs 21. Order 9. Monoecia Monodelphia.

* THE *Male* flowers are collected in an ovate Katkin.

The *Calyx*, a common ovate Katkin, compounded with ſparſed flowers, conſiſting of *Scales* which are uniflorous, roundiſh, ſharp-pointed on the fore part, targetted, oppoſite and in number about twenty.

The *Corolla* none.

The *Filaments* are wanting; but four *Antheræ* are joined, in their ſtead, to each ſcale of the katkin.

* The *Female* flowers are collected in a roundiſh cone, on the ſame plant.

The

The *Calyx*, a common cone, which is compounded of from eight to ten florets, consisting of *Scales*, which are uniflorous, opposite, ovate, convex beneath and gaping.

The *Corolla* none.

The *Germen* is scarce observable. In the place, perhaps, of Styles, there are numerous dots within each calycine scale, which are truncated, and concave at the apex.

The *Seed-vessel*, none but the globose cone, which is shut, but gaping with orbiculate, angled, and targetted scales.

The *Seed* is a nut, which is angled, sharp-pointed, and small.

The Species *with us, are*,

1. CUPRESSUS disticha. *Virginian deciduous Cypress-Tree.*

This grows naturally in swampy, low ground; and becomes a lofty tree, of seventy or eighty feet in height, and three or four feet in diameter; dividing, towards the top, into many branches, clothed with small linear leaves, coming out upon all sides, yet inclining to but two sides of the small branches; and falling off in the autumn. The cones, of this kind, are roundish and near an inch in diameter. The timber is valuable for many uses, affording great quantities of boards, shingles, &c.

2. CUPRESSUS Thyoides. *Maryland Blue-berried Cypress.*

This, by some means, has obtained the name of a dwarf, yet it becomes a large tree, nearly equal in height and diameter to the former. The branches are covered with small ever-green leaves, much resembling those of the Arbor Vitæ. The cones are about the size of Juniper-berries, a little angular and having many cells. The timber of this is softer than the other kind and applied to more general use, being

being durable and not liable to be eaten by worms; it affords excellent planks, &c. for ſhip building; alſo poſts, rails, boards, ſhingles, &c. &c. and to it our dairy women are indebted for tubs, pails, churns, &c.

DIOSPYROS.

The DATE PLUM, or PERSIMMON TREE.

Claſs 23. Order 2. Polygamia Dioecia.

* THE *Hermaphrodite* female.

The *Empalement* is compoſed of one leaf, four-cleft, large, obtuſe and permanent.

The *Corolla*, of one petal, pitcher-ſhape, larger, and four-cleft; the diviſions acute and ſpreading.

The *Filaments* are eight, briſtly, ſhort and lightly inſerted in the receptacle. The *Antheræ* are oblong and effœte.

The *Germen* is roundiſh. The *Style* one, half four-cleft, permanent and longer than the ſtamina. The *Stigmas* are obtuſe and two-cleft.

The *Seed-veſſel* is a berry, which is globous, large, eight-cell'd, and ſitting on the large ſpreading calyx.

The *Seeds* are ſolitary, roundiſh, compreſſed, and very hard.

* The *Male* in diſtinct plants.

The *Empalement* conſiſts of one leaf, four-cleft, acute, erect, and ſmall.

The *Corolla* of one petal, pitcher-ſhape, coriaceous, four-cornered and four cleft: the diviſions are roundiſh and revolute.

The *Filaments* are eight, very ſhort and inſerted in the receptacle. The *Antheræ* are double, long, and acute; the interior ſhorteſt.

The *Piſtillum*, is the rudiment of a germen.

The Species *with us, but one,* viz.

DIOSPYROS virginiana. *Virginian Perſimmon Tree.*

This grows naturally in moiſt clayey ground, in Pennſylvania and Maryland, as well as Virginia; riſing

ing to the height of twenty feet or more, ſending out many ſhortiſh branches, garniſhed with entire, oblong, pointed leaves; the flowers are produced upon the ſmall branches, making but little appearance, and are ſucceeded by large, globular or oblong fruit, which when fully ripe has a ſweet agreeable taſte. A full grown tree will often yield two buſhels or more of fruit, which upon diſtillation will afford as many gallons of Spirits, allowed to be equal in taſte and flavour to Weſt India Rum. Our countrymen have not enough attended to this, but in ſome places they brew of them a very good Beer. There appears to be varieties of this, ſome with early ripe large fruit, others with ſmaller and late ripe.

DIRCA.

LEATHER WOOD.

Claſs 8. Order 1. Octandria Monogynia.

THE *Empalement* is wanting.

The *Corolla* is one petal'd and clubb'd. The tube is more bellied above. The border none, the margin unequal.

The *Filaments* are eight, capillary, inſerted in the middle of the tube, and longer than the corolla. The *Antheræ* are roundiſh and erect.

The *Germen* is ovate, with an oblique top. The *Style* is thread-form, longer than the ſtamina and curved at the top. The *Stigma* is ſimple.

The *Seed-veſſel* is a berry of one cell.

The *Seed* is one.

There is but one Species *of this Genus*, viz.

DIRCA paluſtris. *Virginian Marſh Leatherwood.*

This is a low ſhrub, growing in moiſt ſhady places, ſeldom riſing more than three or four feet high, ſpreading

ſpreading into a head, with many ſmall and very flexible branches, covered with a light coloured bark, and cloathed with oval ſmooth leaves, of a pale green colour. The flowers are produced at the extreme ends of the former year's ſhoots; they are of an herbaceous colour and make but little appearance, but are ſucceeded by oval berries, changing ſomewhat yellowiſh when ripe.

EPIGÆA.

TRAILING ARBUTUS.

Claſs 10. Order 1. Decandria Monogynia.

THE *Empalement* is double, approximated, and permanent.
The *exterior* conſiſts of three leaves, which are ovate-lanced, and ſharp pointed; the exterior largeſt.
The *interior* is five-parted and erect; a little longer than the exterior: the leaf-lets are lanced and ſharp pointed.

The *Corolla* is compoſed of one pitcher-form petal. The tube is cylindrical, rather longer than the calyx, and hairy within. The border is ſpreading and five-parted, with ovate-oblong lobes.

The *Filaments* are ten, thread-form, the length of the tube and affixed to the baſe of the corolla. The *Antheræ* are oblong and acute.

The *Germen* is globoſe and villous. The *Style* is thread-form, and the length of the ſtamina. The *Stigma* is obtuſe and ſomewhat five-cleft.

The *Seed-veſſel* is a capſule, ſomewhat roundiſh, depreſſed, five ſided, five cell'd, and five valv'd.

The *Seeds* are many and roundiſh. The receptable large and five-parted.

There is but one Species *of this Genus*, viz.

EPIGÆA repens. *Trailing Arbutus.*

This grows naturally upon northern hills, or mountains, with trailing ſhrubby ſtalks, putting out roots

at

at their joints. The leaves are oblong, rough and waved on their edges. The flowers are produced at the ends of the branches, in loofe panicles, and are of a white colour, mixed with red, dividing at the top into five parts, and fpreading open in form of a ftar.

EUONYMUS.

The SPINDLE TREE.

Clafs 5. Order 1. Pentandria Monogynia.

THE *Empalement* is compofed of one leaf, five-parted, and plane: the divifions are roundifh and concave.

The *Corolla* confifts of five petals, ovate, plane, fpreading and longer than the calyx.

The *Filaments* are five, awl-fhaped, erect, fhorter than the corolla, and placed on the germen as a receptacle. The *Antheræ* are twin.

The *Germen* is fharp pointed. The *Style* is fhort and fimple. The *Stigma* is obtufe.

The *Seed-veffel* is a capfule, fucculent, coloured, pentagonal, with five angles, five cells and five valves.

The *Seeds* are folitary, ovate and covered with a berry'd Arillus.

Obf. In fome fpecies one fifth part of the fructification is taken away.

The Species *with us, are,*

1. EUONYMUS carolinenfis. *Carolinian Spindle Tree.*

This fhrub grows to the height of eight or ten feet, dividing into many oppofite branches, the young fhoots are fomewhat quadrangular and marked longitudinally, with green ftripes. The leaves are placed oppofite, and are oval, fharp pointed, and finely and flightly fawed on their edges, of a deep green

green colour. The footſtalks of the flowers come out from the boſom of the leaves of the young ſhoots, and are generally divided into three parts towards their extremities, the middle diviſion ſuſtaining one, and the two ſide ones, each three flowers; having four deep purple coloured petals, expanding in form of a croſs, and four ſtamina; theſe are ſucceeded by angular furrowed ſeed veſſels, of a beautiful pale red colour when ripe, making a fine appearance after the leaves are fallen off.

2. EUONYMUS latifolius. *Broad-leaved Spindle Tree.*

This ſhrub very much reſembles the former, except the leaves being broader and longer, and of a paler green colour, turning reddiſh before they fall off. The ſeed-veſſels are rather larger and rounder at the corners or angles, and of ſomewhat paler colour, as are alſo the flowers.

3. EUONYMUS ſempervirens. *Ever-green Spindle Tree.*

This is of ſmaller growth than either of the former, ſeldom riſing above ſix or ſeven feet, and dividing into many oppoſite branches, towards the top, which are of a greener colour, and more angular than the other kinds, and garniſhed with narrower leaves, of a cloſer texture. The flowers are produced in manner of the former, except each footſtalk ſuſtaining generally but three flowers, having five petals, which are of a paler colour, and rounder than either of the former; and are ſucceeded by roundiſh capſules cloſely ſet with ſmall protuberances, turning of a fine red colour when ripe, and opening into

four

four or five parts, difclofing its feeds hanging by fine white threads. This makes a very beautiful appearance in autumn when its fruit are ripe; and from their red appearance obtained the name of the Burning Bufh. The young plants retain their leaves all winter. All the fpecies grow naturally in moift, fhaded places.

FAGUS.

The BEECH-TREE.

Clafs 21. Order 8. Monoecia Polyandria.

* THE *Male* flowers are affixed to an Amentaceous receptacle. The *Calyx* is an *Empalement* of one leaf, bell-fhaped, and five-cleft.

The *Corolla* none.

The *Filaments* are many (about twelve) the length of the calyx, and briftly. The *Antheræ* are oblong.

* The *Female* flowers are contained in buds upon the fame plant.

The *Calyx*, an *Empalement* of one leaf, four-toothed, erect and acute.

The *Corolla* none.

The *Germen* is covered by the calyx. The *Styles* are three, awl-fhaped. The *Stigmas* are fimple and reflexed.

The *Seed-veffel* is a capfule (formerly the calyx) which is roundifh, large, fet round with foft fpines; with one cell and four valves.

The *Seeds* are two nuts, which are ovate, triangular, three valved and fharp-pointed.

Obf. The Male flowers of the Beech are difpofed in a globular form; thofe of the Chefnut in a cylindrical.

We have but one Species *of this Genus, befides the Chefnut and Chinquepin, which are fomewhat improperly joined with it,* viz.

FAGUS

FAGUS Sylvatica atro-punicea. *American Beech Tree.*

This grows naturally in low, bottom grounds, by river ſides, riſing ſometimes to the height of forty or fifty feet, and to fifteen or eighteen inches in diameter, generally ſending out many long branches, garniſhed with very thin, oval, ſpear-ſhaped leaves, ſawed on their edges, and remaining late upon the branches. The nuts are eaten by ſwine. The wood is hard and cloſe grained, and uſed for making laſts, joiner's tools, &c.

FAGUS-CASTANEA.

The CHESNUT TREE.

THE Characters are nearly the ſame of the Beech, except the Male flowers being diſpoſed in cylindrical katkins. The *Styles* more in number and briſtly. The *Capſules* much larger, round, and ſet very thick with long prickly Spines; containing from one to four or five, but generally two or three nuts, filled with ſweet kernel.

The Species *of Cheſnut, with us, are,*

1. FAGUS-CASTANEA dentata. *American Cheſnut Tree.*

This often becomes a large tree, growing to the height of ſixty or eighty feet, and to four or five feet in diameter, ſending out but few branches, garniſhed with long ſpear-ſhaped leaves, toothed or notched on their edges. The timber is uſed much for rails, ſplitting free and out-laſting moſt of our Oaks. The kernel of the nuts are dried and uſed by ſome as a ſubſtitute for Coffee. The wood is alſo burnt

burnt into coals for the uſe of blackſmiths, &c. but not much eſteemed for common fuel.

2. FAGUS-CASTANEA pumila. *Dwarf Cheſnut Tree, or Chinquepin.*

This ſeldom riſes above eight, ten, or twelve feet, otherwiſe much reſembling the Cheſnut in the appearance of its branches and leaves. Its fruit capſules are ſmall, and generally contain but one conical ſhaped nut. It grows naturally in a light gravelly ſoil.

FOTHERGILLA.

FOTHERGILLA.

Claſs 13. Order 2. Polyandria Digynia.

THE *Empalement* is of one leaf, hairy, and five-toothed at the margin.

The *Corolla* is wanting.

The *Filaments* from ſixteen to eighteen, inſerted in the calyx, long, incurved and leſſened towards the baſe. The *Antheræ* are minute.

The *Germen* is oblong and villoſe, ending in two acute *Styles.*

The *Seed-veſſel* is a capſule, oblong, of two cells and covered by the calyx.

The *Seeds* are ſingle and oblong.

The Species *with us,*

FOTHERGILLA Gardeni. *Carolinian Fothergilla.*

This ſmall, but beautiful flowering ſhrub grows naturally in Carolina, on the borders of ſavannahs, or near ponds of water; ſpreading much by its roots. The ſtalks are ſlender, riſing to the height of two or or three feet, generally ſeveral from one root, with ſmall, alternate, divaricated branches. The leaves are oval, ſomewhat toothed towards the apex, and placed alternate. The flowers are produced in ſpikes terminating the ſtalks; they are ſeſſile, and each furniſhed with a bractea or floral leaf, which is ovate, rough externally, longer than the empalement and ſitting cloſe at their baſe; they are produced early in the ſpring and being thick ſet, make a beautiful appearance with their long, ſnowy white ſtamina. The fruit or ſeed-veſſel very much reſembles that of the Hamamalis or Witch Hazel, but is much ſmaller.

This, in ſome late Catalogues, has been called *Youngſonia*, in honour of William Young, Botaniſt, of Pennſylvania; but by Dr. Linnæus, *Fothergilla* in honour of the late Dr. Fothergill of London. It was firſt ſent to Europe, from Carolina, by John Bartram, to his friend P. Collinſon, by the title of Gardenia.

FRANKLINIA.

FRANKLINIA.

Claſs 16. Order 5. Monadelphia Polyandria.

THE *Empalement* is of one leaf, five-cleft; the diviſions roundiſh.

The *Corolla* conſiſts of five petals, large, ſpreading, roundiſh, narrowed towards the claw, and joined at the baſe.

The *Filaments* are numerous, awl-ſhaped, joined beneath in a cylinder, and inſerted in the corolla. The *Antheræ* are twin.

The *Germen* is roundiſh, lightly furrowed. The *Style* cylindrical and longer than the ſtamina. The *Stigma* obtuſe and rayed.

The *Seed-veſſel*, a roundiſh nut with five cells.

The *Seeds* are wedge-form, and ſeveral in each cell.

The Species *one*, viz.

FRANKLINIA alatamaha. *Franklinia.*

(Bartram's Catalogue.)

This beautiful flowering, tree-like ſhrub, riſes with an erect trunk to the height of about twenty feet; dividing into branches, alternately diſpoſed. The leaves are oblong, narrowed towards the baſe, ſawed on their edges, placed alternately, and ſitting cloſe to the branches. The flowers are produced towards the extremity of the branches, ſitting cloſe at the boſom of the leaves; they are often five inches in diameter when fully expanded; compoſed of five large, roundiſh, ſpreading petals, ornamented in the center with a tuft or crown of gold coloured ſtamina; and poſſeſſed with the fragrance of a China Orange. This newly diſcovered, rare, and elegant flowering ſhrub, was firſt obſerved by John Bartram when on botanical reſearches, on the Alatamaha river in Georgia, Anno 1760; but was not brought into Pennſylvania till about fifteen years after, when his ſon William Bartram, employed in the like purſuits, reviſited the place where it had been before obſerved, and had the pleaſing proſpect of beholding it in its native ſoil, poſſeſſed with all its floral charms; and bearing ripe ſeeds at the ſame time; ſome of which he collected and brought home, and raiſed ſeveral plants therefrom, which in four years time flowered, and in one year after perfected ripe ſeeds.

It ſeems nearly allied to the Gordonia, to which it has, in ſome late Catalogues, been joined: but William Bartram, who firſt introduced it, believing it to be a new Genus, has choſen to honour it with the name of that patron of ſciences, and truly great and

and distinguished character, Dr. Benjamin Franklin. The trivial name is added from the river, where alone it has been observed to grow naturally. It delights in a loose, sandy and moist soil.

FRAXINUS.

The ASH-TREE.

Class 23. Order 2. Polygamia Dioecia.

THE Flowers are *Hermaphrodite* and *Female* on different trees.
* The *Hermaphrodite*:

The *Calyx* none; or an *Empalement* of one leaf, four-parted, erect, acute, and small.

The *Corolla* none; or of four petals, linear, long, acute, and erect.

The *Filaments* are two, erect and shorter than the corolla. The *Antheræ* are erect, oblong, and four furrowed.

The *Germen* is ovate and compressed. The *Style* cylindrical and erect. The *Stigma* thickish and two cleft.

The *Seed-vessel* none besides the crust of the seed.

The *Seed* is lanced, compressed-membranaceous and of one cell.

* The *Female* are the same in every part except wanting the stamina.

The Species *are*,

1. FRAXINUS americana. *Carolinian or Red Ash.*

This grows to the height of twenty or thirty feet, dividing into several branches, the small ones of which are generally opposite; the leaves are composed of three or four pair of lobes, terminated by an odd one, which are egg-shaped and pointed, their upper surface of a light green colour, their under covered with short white downy hairs. The seeds are broad and of a light colour.

2. FRAXINUS alba. *American White Aſh.*

This tree grows ſometimes to the height of forty or fifty feet, and to eighteen inches or more in diameter. It grows much after the manner of the former, only the leaves are broader, and the ſeeds narrower. The timber of this is uſed much by Wheelwrights, Chaiſe-makers, &c. for making ſhafts, rimming of wheels, &c.

3. FRAXINUS Nigra. *Black Aſh.*

This kind grows in moiſt places, riſing to the height of thirty feet or more, covered with a rough, lightiſh coloured bark, and ſending out but few branches. The leaves are chiefly produced at the ends of the branches, and are generally compoſed of four pair of lobes, and an odd one, which are ſhaped like thoſe of the other kinds, but are ſmaller and finely ſawed on their edges. The ſeeds or keys are broad and flat, and of equal width their whole length.

4. FRAXINUS pennſylvanica. *Pennſylvanian Sharp-keyed Aſh.*

This kind often grows to the height of thirty feet or more, and is generally thick ſet with branches towards the top, having leaves much reſembling the White Aſh. The ſeeds grow in large panicles, thick ſet upon the ſides of the branches, near their extremities: they are longer and narrower than any of the other kinds, almoſt terminating in a point at their baſe. This alſo affords a valuable wood, which is uſed for the ſame purpoſes as that of the White Aſh.

The

The inside bark and keys of Ash, are accounted good to promote urine.

GAULTHERIA.

GAULTHERIA, or MOUNTAIN TEA.

Class 10. Order 1. Decandria Monogynia.

THE *Empalement* is double, approximate and permanent.
The *exterior* two leaved and shorter: the leaves semi-ovate, concave and obtuse.
The *interior* one leaved, five-cleft and bell-shaped: the segments semi-ovate.

The *Corolla* is monopetalous, ovate and half five cleft: the border small and revolute.
A *Nectarium* of ten corpuscules, which are awl-shaped, erect, very short, and surrounding the germen within the stamina.

The *Filaments* are ten, awl-shaped, incurved, shorter than the corolla, and inserted in the receptacle. The *Antheræ* are two horned: the horns bifid.

The *Germen* is roundish and depressed. The *Style* cylindrical and the length of the corolla. The *Stigma* is obtuse.

The *Seed-vessel* is a capsule, roundish, obtuse five-sided, depressed, five cell'd, and five valv'd; covered on all sides by the interior empalement, and becoming a roundish coloured berry, pervious at the apex.

The *Seeds* are many, somewhat ovate, angled and bony.

There is but one Species *of this Genus*, viz.

GAULTHERIA procumbens. *Canadian Gaultheria, or Mountain Tea.*

This is a very small shrubby plant, with slender stems, seldom rising above five or six inches in height; having, at their tops, four or five oval ever-green leaves, which are marked with a few small points or serratures upon their edges. The flowers come out from the bosom of the leaves, of a white colour, and

and are succeeded by small berries of a red colour when ripe. The leaves have been used as a substitute for Bohea Tea, whence the name of Mountain Tea.

GLEDITSIA.

TRIPLE-THORNED ACACIA, or HONEY LOCUST.

Class 23. Order 2. Polygamia Dioecia.

THE Flowers are *Male* and *Hermaphrodite* upon the same plant, and *Female* upon a different plant.

* The *Male* are in a long, compact, cylindrical katkin.

The *Calyx*; a proper empalement of four leaves: the leaves spreading, small and acute.

The *Corolla* consists of three petals, roundish, sessile, spreading, and cup form.

A *Nectarium*, top-shaped, to whose borders the remaining parts of fructification grow.

The *Filaments* are six, thread-form, and the length of the corolla. The *Antheræ* are incumbent, oblong, compressed and twin.

* The *Hermaphrodite* are in the same katkin with the male flowers, and for the most part terminal.

The *Calyx*, an empalement, four leaved, as in the male.

The *Corolla*, four petals, as in the male.

The *Nectarium* as in the male.

The *Stamina* as in the male.

The *Pistillum*, *Seed-vessel*, and *Seeds* as in the female.

* The *Female Flowers* are in a loose katkin, in a different plant.

The *Calyx*; a proper empalement, as in the male, but five leaved.

The *Corolla*, five petals, which are long, acute, and somewhat spreading.

The *Nectaria* are two, very short, like the filaments.

The *Germen* is broad, compressed, and longer than the corolla. The *Style* is short and reflexed. The *Stigma* is thick and the length of the style, to which it is adjoined, growing hairy above.

The *Seed-vessel* is a legumen or pod, very large, broad, and much compressed, with many transverse partitions: with isthmuses filled with pulp.

The *Seeds* are solitary, roundish, hard and shining.

The

The Species *with, us are,*

1. GLEDITSIA ſpinoſa. *Triple-thorned Acacia, or Honey Locuſt.*

This tree grows naturally in a rich ſoil, riſing to the height of thirty or forty feet, dividing into many branches, which, together with the trunk, are armed with long pithy ſpines of five or ſix inches in length, ſending off laternal ones, ſome of which are nearly the ſame length, and generally triple thorned. The branches are garniſhed with winged leaves, compoſed of ten, or more pair of ſmall lobes, ſitting cloſe to the midrib, of a lucid green colour. The flowers come out from the ſides of the young branches in form of katkins, of an herbaceous colour, and are ſucceeded by crooked, compreſſed pods, from nine or ten to ſixteen or eighteen inches in length, and about an inch and a half or two inches in breadth, of which near one half is filled with a ſweet pulp, the other containing many ſeeds in ſeparate cells. The pods, from the ſweetneſs of their pulp, are uſed to brew in beer.

2. GLEDITSIA aquatica. *Water Acacia.*

This ſort grows naturally in Carolina, and hath much the appearance of the firſt, but hath fewer ſpines, which are very ſhort. The leaves are alſo ſmaller and the pods oval, containing but one ſeed.

GLYCINE.

PERENNIAL KIDNEY BEAN.

Claſs 17. Order 3. Diadelphia Decandria.

THE *Empalement* is of one leaf, compreſſed and two lipped: the upper lip emarginate and obtuſe: the lower, longer, acute, and three-cleft; the middle diviſion longeſt.

The

The *Corolla* papilionaceous, or butterfly ſhaped.

The *Standard* inverſe heart-ſhaped, the ſides deflexed, the back gibbous, the apex emarginate, ſtraight and bent from the keel.

The *Wings* oblong, ovate towards the top, ſmall and bent downwards.

The *Keel* linear, hooked, broader and obtuſe towards the point, and bent upwards, preſſing againſt the ſtandard.

The *Filaments* are diadelphous, or one ſingle, and nine conjoined; a little dividing at the top, and revolute. The *Antheræ* are ſimple.

The *Germen* is oblong. The *Style* cylindrical, bending back in a ſpire. The *Stigma* obtuſe.

The *Seed-veſſel* an oblong legumen or pod.

The *Seeds* kidney form.

Obſ. Glycine fruteſcens has legumens or pods of two cells.

The ſhrubby Species *with us, is one,* viz.

GLYCINE fruteſcens. *Carolinian Shrubby Kidney Bean.*

This grows naturally in Carolina, riſing with twining ſhrubby ſtems, when ſupported, to the height of ten or fifteen feet. The leaves are winged, and compoſed of about five pair of ſmall, oval, pointed pinnæ or lobes, ſmooth and of a pale green on their upper ſurface, but lighter underneath, having their edges a little reflexed and hairy. The flowers terminate the branches in a cloſe, erect racemus or bunch; they are of a purpliſh blue colour, and are ſucceeded by long cylindrical pods of two cells, ſhaped like thoſe of the ſcarlet Kidney Bean.

GUILANDINA.

GUILANDINA.

The BONDUC, or NICKAR TREE.

Claſs 10. Order 1. Decandria Monogynia.

THE *Empalement* is one leaved, bell-ſhape: the border five parted, equal, and ſpreading.

The *Corolla* conſiſts of five petals, lanced, concave, ſquat, equal, ſomewhat larger than the calyx and inſerted in its chaps.

The *Filaments* are ten, awl-ſhaped, erect, inſerted in, and ſhorter than the calyx: the alternate leſs. The *Antheræ* are obtuſe and incumbent.

The *Germen* is oblong. The *Style* is thread-form and the length of the ſtamina. The *Stigma* is ſimple.

The *Seed-veſſel* is a legumen or pod, which is rhomboid, convex on the upper ſuture, bellied-compreſſed, of one cell, diſtinct, with tranſverſe partitions.

The *Seeds* are bony, globoſe-compreſſed, and ſolitary between the partitions.

Obſ. A ſpecies of this genus is dioecious.

The Species *with us,*

GUILANDINA dioica. *Canadian dioiceous Bonduc, or Nickar Tree.*

This tree is ſaid to riſe, with an erect ſtem, to the height of thirty feet or more, dividing into many branches, covered with a bluiſh aſh-coloured, ſmooth bark, garniſhed with large winged leaves, the lobes of which are ranged alternately, and are oval ſhaped, very ſmooth and entire. I have lately received ſeveral ſeeds from Kentucky, ſuppoſed to be of this tree, where it is ſaid to grow plenty, and is called the Coffee or Mahogany tree.

HALESIA.

HALESIA.

HALESIA, or SILVER-BELL TREE.

Claſs 10. Order 1. Decandria Monogynia.

THE *Empalement* is one leaved, very ſmall, above, four-toothed, and permanent.

The *Corolla* is of one petal, bell'd and bellied: with the mouth four-lobed, obtuſe and ſpreading.

The *Filaments* are twelve (rarely ſixteen) awl-ſhaped, erect and ſomewhat ſhorter than the corolla. The *Antheræ* are oblong, obtuſe and erect.

The *Germen* is oblong and beneath. The *Style* is thread-form and longer than the corolla. The *Stigma* is ſimple.

The *Seed-veſſel* is a nut which is barked, oblong, narrow towards each end, four cornered with membranaceous angles, and two cell'd.

The *Seeds* are ſolitary.

The Species *are,*

1. HALESIA diptera. *Two-winged fruited Haleſia.*

This grows naturally in Carolina, to the height of twelve or fifteen feet. The bark is beautifully variegated or ſtreaked, much like the ſtriped Maple. The leaves are large and egg-ſhaped, having ſmooth footſtalks. The fruit is ſharp-pointed, having two oppoſite, large wings, and two very ſmall.

2. HALESIA tetraptera. *Four-winged fruited Haleſia.*

This likewiſe grows in Carolina, and has much the appearance of the former, except the leaves are much ſmaller, a little ſawed on their edges and downy

downy underneath, with glandular footſtalks. The flowers are produced upon the ſmall branches, ſometimes ſingly, but often three or four together, upon pretty long footſtalks; they are bell-ſhaped and pendulous, of a white colour, and are ſucceeded by ſharp-pointed fruit, having four wings.

HAMAMELIS.

WITCH HAZEL.

Claſs 4. Order 2. Tetrandria Digynia.

THE *Calyx* conſiſts of an Involucrum, three-leaved, and three flowered: the two interior leaves are roundiſh, leſs, and obtuſe; the third outer one is larger and lance-ſhaped.

A double Empalement: the exterior two leaved, leſs and roundiſh; the interior four leaved and erect; the leaves oblong, obtuſe, and equal.

The *Corolla* has four petals, which are linear, equal, very long, obtuſe, and reflexed.

And a *Nectarium*, of four leaf-lets, truncated, and adjoined to the corolla.

The *Filaments* are four, linear, and ſhorter than the calyx. The *Antheræ* two horned and reflexed.

The *Germen* is ovate and villoſe, ending in two Styles, the length of the Stamina. The *Stigmas* are headed.

The *Seed-veſſel* none.

The *Seed*, a nut which is ovate, half covered with the calyx, obtuſe and furrowed on each ſide at the apex with ſmall horizontal two horned horns; with two cells and two valves.

We have but one Species *of this Genus*, viz.

HAMAMELIS virginiana. *Virginian Witch Hazel.*

This ſhrub grows naturally in many parts of North America. It hath ſpreading roots, generally ſending up ſeveral ſtalks or ſtems to the height of eight or or ten feet, dividing into ſeveral branches, furniſhed with oval leaves irregularly notched on their edges, and ſmooth on their upper ſides, but downy underneath. The footſtalks of the flowers come out ſingly upon the ſmall branches, each generally ſupporting three flowers, of an herbaceous colour, and making but little appearance, but remarkable for being in bloom late in the fall after the leaves drop off.

HEDERA.

IVY.

Claſs 5. Order 1. Pentandria Monogynia.

THE *Calyx* conſiſts of an Involucrum of a ſimple umbel, very ſmall and many toothed.

And an *Empalement* very ſmall, five toothed and ſurrounding the germen.

The *Corolla* has five petals, oblong and ſpreading, with incurved tops.

The *Filaments* are five, awl-ſhaped, erect and the length of the corolla. The *Antheræ* are bifid at the baſe, and incumbent.

The *Germen* is top ſhaped, ſurrounded by the receptacle. The *Style* is ſimple and very ſhort. The *Stigma* is ſimple.

The *Seed-veſſel* is a globoſe berry of one cell.

The *Seeds* are five, large, on one ſide gibbous, on the other angled.

We have but one Species *Native of America*, viz.

HEDERA quinquefolia. *American Ivy, or Virginian Creeper.*

This hath a climing ſtem, attaching itſelf to any neighbouring ſupport, and riſing often to the height of thirty, forty or fifty feet, ſending off branches, furniſhed with leaves compoſed of five lobes joined

at

at their baſe, which are egg-ſhaped and ſawed on their edges, having a pretty long common footſtalk. This has been uſed to plant againſt walls and houſes to cover them, but the leaves falling off in winter, the plants make but a poor appearance at that time.

HIPPOPHAË.

SEA BUCK-THORN, or SALLOW-THORN.

Claſs 22. Order 4. Dioecia Tetrandria.

THE flowers are Male and Female on different plants.

* The *Male*.

The *Empalement* is one leaved, biparted, bivalve, entire at the bottom: the diviſions are roundiſh, obtuſe, concave and erect, meeting with their tops, but gaping at their ſides.

The *Corolla* is wanting.

The *Filaments* are four, very ſhort. The *Antheræ* are oblong, angled, and almoſt the length of the calyx.

* The *Female*.

The *Empalement* is one leaved, oblong-ovate, tubulous, clubbed, with a two cleft mouth, and deciduous.

The *Corolla* none.

The *Germen* is roundiſh, and ſmall. The *Style* is ſimple and very ſhort. The *Stigma* thickiſh, oblong, erect, and double the length of the calyx.

The *Seed-veſſel* is a globoſe berry of one cell.

The *Seed* one, roundiſh.

There is but one Species, *with us*, viz.

HIPPOPHAË canadienſis. *Canadian Sea-Buck-Thorn.*

This riſes with ſhrubby ſtalks to the height of eight or ten feet, ſending out many irregular branches, having a brown bark, ſilvered over, and garniſhed with very narrow ſpear-ſhaped leaves, of a dark green on their upper ſide, but hoary underneath, and reflexed

reflexed on their edges like the Rofemary. The flowers come out from the fides of the young branches, fitting very clofe; the male growing in fmall clufters, but the female coming out fingly; thefe open in July and make but little appearance; they are fucceeded by roundifh berries, which ripen in autumn, and are faid to be purgative.

HYDRANGEA.

HYDRANGEA.

Clafs 10. Order 2. Decandria Digynia.

THE *Empalement* is one leaved, five toothed, permanent, and fmall.

The *Corolla* confifts of five petals, equal, roundifh, and larger than the calyx.

The *Filaments* are ten, longer than the corolla, the alternate of which are longer. The *Antheræ* are roundifh and twin.

The *Germen* is roundifh and beneath. The *Styles* are two, fhort, and diftant. The *Stigmas* are obtufe and permanent.

The *Seed-veffel* is a capfule, roundifh, twin, two beaked with the double ftyle, angled with many nerves, crowned with the calyx, two cell'd, with a tranfverfe partition, and gaping with a paffage between the horns.

The *Seeds* are numerous, angled, fharp pointed, and very fmall.

There is but one Species *of this Genus*, viz.

HYDRANGEA frutefcens. *Virginian Shrubby Hydrangea.*

This hath a fpreading woody root, from which are produced, generally feveral foft, pithy, ligneous ftalks, rifing to the height of about three feet, garnifhed at each joint with two oblong, heart-fhaped, pointed leaves, fawed on their edges, and having many veins. The flowers are produced in form of a coa corymbus, at the tops of the ſtalks, they are of a white colour, and are ſucceeded by ſmall capſules.

HYPERICUM.

St. JOHN's WORT.

Claſs 18. Order 3. Polyadelphia Polyandria.

THE *Empalement* is five parted: the diviſions are ſomewhat ovate, convex, and permanent.
The *Corolla* has five petals, oblong-ovate, obtuſe, ſpreading, and marked according to the motion of the ſun.
The *Filaments* are numerous, capillary, joined at the baſe into five or three parts or bodies. The *Antheræ* are ſmall.
The *Germen* is roundiſh. The *Styles* are three (ſometimes one, two, and five) ſimple, diſtant, and the length of the ſtamina.
The *Stigmas* are ſimple.
The *Seed-veſſel* is a roundiſh capſule; with cells according to the number of the Styles.
The *Seeds* are many and oblong.

The Species *growing ſhrubby, with us,*

HYPERICUM kalmianum. *Virginian Shrubby Hypericum.*

This grows naturally in low wet places, riſing with ſhrubby ſtalks to the height of three or four feet, with oppoſite angular branches. The leaves are ſmooth and ſhaped like thoſe of Roſemary or Lavender. The flowers terminate the branches in ſmall divided cluſters of three or ſeven flowers; they have each five very ſlender ſtyles, and are ſucceeded by oval, pointed capſules, filled with ſmall ſeeds.

ILEX.

I L E X.

The HOLLY-TREE.

Clafs 4. Order 3. Tetrandria Tetragynia.

THE *Empalement* is four toothed, very fmall and permanent.
The *Corolla* confifts of one petal, four-parted and plane: the divifions are roundifh, concave, fpreading, pretty large, and cohering by claws.
The *Filaments* are four, awl-fhaped, and fhorter than the corolla. The *Antheræ* are fmall.
The *Germen* is roundifh. The *Style* none. The *Stigmas* are four and obtufe.
The *Seed-veffel* is a berry, roundifh and four cell'd.
The *Seeds* are folitary, bony, oblong, obtufe, gibbous on one fide and angled on the other.
Obf. The flowers are in fome fpecies male upon one plant, and female and hermaphrodite upon a different plant.

The Species *with us, are,*

1. ILEX Aquifolium. *American Common Holly.*

This grows in Maryland, New Jerfey, &c. generally in moift ground, rifing to the height of fifteen or twenty feet, with an erect ftem, covered with a greyifh coloured fmooth bark, and furnifhed with pretty many branches, which are garnifhed with thick, hard, ever-green leaves, waved on their edges and indented, each point terminating in a ftiff prickly fpine. The flowers are produced upon pretty long footftalks, often three parted from the fides of the branches, of a white colour, having often five or fix ftamina, and the corolla divided into as many parts, and are fucceeded by roundifh berries, which when full ripe are red. Of the bark of common Holly is made Birdlime, which is better than that made of Miffletoe.

2. ILEX

2. Ilex Caſſine. *Dahoon, or Carolinian Holly.*

This grows naturally in Carolina, riſing with an upright branching ſtem to the height of eighteen or twenty feet. The bark of the ſtem is of a brown colour, but that of the branches and young ſhoots green and ſmooth. The leaves are ſpear-ſhaped, above four inches long and one and a quarter broad toward the baſe, of a light green colour and thick conſiſtence, with their upper parts ſawed on the edges, each ſerrature ending in a ſmall ſharp ſpine. The flowers come out in thick cluſters from the ſides of the branches, they are white and like thoſe of the common Holly, but ſmaller, and are ſucceeded by ſmall roundiſh red berries.

3. Ilex canadenſis. *Canadian, or Hedge-hog Holly.*

The leaves of this kind are not ſo long as thoſe of the Common Holly, but are armed with ſtronger ſpines ſtanding cloſer together, their upper ſurfaces are alſo ſet very cloſe with ſhort prickles, from whence it obtained the name of Hedge-hog Holly. It grows naturally in Canada. There are ſaid to be two varieties of this with variegated leaves, one of which is yellow, the other white.

I T E A.

I T E A.

Claſs 5. Order 1. Pentandria Monogynia.

THE *Empalement* is one leaved, five cleft, erect, ſharp pointed, very ſmall, and permanent: the diviſions are acute and coloured.

The

The *Corolla* has five petals, lance-ſhaped, long and inſerted in the calyx.

The *Filaments* are five, awl-ſhaped, erect, the length of the corolla, and inſerted into the calyx. The *Antheræ* are roundiſh and incumbent.

The *Germen* is ovate. The *Style* is cylindrical, permanent, and the length of the Stamina. The *Stigma* is obtuſe.

The *Seed-veſſel* is a capſule. ovate, much longer than the calyx, pointed with the ſtyle, with one cell and two valves, of two joined together, gaping at the top.

The *Seeds* are numerous, very ſmall, oblong, and ſhining.

There is but one Species *of this Genus*, viz.

ITEA virginica. *Virginian Itea.*

This ſhrub grows naturally in Maryland, Virginia, &c. near ſtreams of water, or in moiſt places; riſing to the height of eight or ten feet, and dividing into ſeveral branches, which are garniſhed with ſpear ſhaped leaves, placed alternately, ſlightly ſawed on their edges, and of a light green colour. The flowers are produced at the extremity of the ſame year's ſhoots, in erect ſpikes of three or four inches in length; they are white, and make a fine appearance when in bloom, which is a little before harveſt time.

JUGLANS.

The WALNUT-TREE.

Claſs 21. Order 8. Monoecia Polyandria.

THE *Male* and *Female* Flowers are ſeparate upon the ſame tree.

* The *Male*, are diſpoſed in an oblong katkin.

The *Calyx* is a common katkin, on all ſides imbricate-ſparſed, and cylindrical; conſiſting of ſcales which are uniflorous, ſingly affixed in the exterior center to each corolla, and turned outward.

The *Corolla* is ſix-parted, elliptic, equal, and plane: the diviſions are ſomewhat erect and concave, pedicell'd and inſerted in the interior center of the corolla, and rachis.

The *Filaments* are many, (eighteen) very ſhort. The *Antheræ* are erect, ſharp pointed and the length of the calyx.

* The *Female* are without a katkin, two or three together, and ſitting cloſe, in the ſame plant.

The *Empalement* is four cleft, erect, very ſhort, crowning the germen, and vaniſhing.

The *Corolla* is four parted, acute, erect, and a little larger than the calyx.

The *Germen* is oval, large, and beneath. The *Styles* are two, very ſhort. The *Stigmas* are very large, clubbed, reflexed, and torn above.

The *Seed-veſſel* is a drupe, or capſule, dry, oval, large and one cell'd.

The *Seed* is a nut very large, roundiſh, netted with furrows, and half four cell'd. The *Kernel* is four lobed and variouſly furrowed.

The Species *(or chiefly Varieties according to* Weſton) *with us, are,*

1. JUGLANS nigra. *Round black Virginian Walnut.*

This tree often riſes to the height of fifty or ſixty feet, and to three feet or more in diameter, covered with a dark furrowed bark, and dividing into many branches, furniſhed with winged leaves, compoſed of ten or twelve pair of lobes, and an odd one; theſe are ſmooth, oblong, ſharp pointed and ſawed on their edges; and upon being bruiſed emit a ſtrong aromatic flavour, as doth alſo the external covering of the fruit. The fruit are round, their covering pretty ſmooth, and ſoftiſh when fully ripe. The nuts themſelves are hard, netted and furrowed, containing ſweet oily kernel.

2. JUGLANS nigra oblonga. *Black oblong fruited Walnut.*

This tree refembles the former fo as fcarcely to be diftinguifhed from it, except by its fruit, which is oblong or oval; the fhells or coverings are rougher, harder, and of a deeper green colour. The timber of both forts is much ufed by Joiners, &c. in making tables, drawers, book and clock-cafes, &c. Coffins are alfo generally made of it. The bark, and outer coverings of the nuts, are ufed in dying wool, cloth, &c.

There are perhaps fome other varieties of thefe.

3. JUGLANS oblonga alba. *Butter-nut, or White Walnut.*

This often grows to the height of twenty or thirty feet and to eighteen inches or more in diameter, with a fmooth light coloured bark. The branches are garnifhed with leaves compofed generally of eight or nine pair of lobes and an odd one, which are villofe, oblong egg-fhaped, fharp pointed, flightly ferrated, and larger than thofe of the other kinds. The fruit, when ripe, is villous and covered with a vifcid clammy fubftance, by which it almoft fticks to the fingers when handled. It is long and fomewhat pointed at the ends, and freed of its hull, or covering, is very rough and deeply furrowed, containing a foft, oily, fweet kernel. An extract of the bark of this tree affords a mild and fafe cathartic. The bark and fhells of the nuts dye a good brown colour, fcarcely ever fading.

4. JUGLANS alba acuminata. *Long, ſharp-fruited Hickery Tree.*

This tree grows to the height of forty or fifty feet, and to eighteen inches or two feet in diameter. The leaves are generally compoſed of three or four pair of lobes and an odd one. The nuts with their covers are about two inches in length and above one in diameter. The covers, or hulls, generally open into four parts, diſcloſing their nuts, which are white, hard and thick ſhell'd, having ſeams oppoſite the diviſions of their hulls. The kernel is ſmall and not very ſweet.

5. JUGLANS alba minima. *White, or Pig-nut Hickery.*

This generally grows pretty large, ſometimes to the height of eighty feet or more, and above two feet in diameter. The bark of young trees is ſmooth, but when older becomes rough and furrowed. The leaves are generally compoſed of five pair of lobes and an odd one, which are moſtly narrower than thoſe of many other kinds. The fruit is ſmall and roundiſh, and covered with a very thin huſk or covering, opening in diviſions. The ſhell of the nut is alſo very thin, and eaſily cracked with the teeth; the kernel plump and full but very bitter. The timber of this is not much eſteemed.

6. JUGLANS alba odorata. *Balſam Hickery.*

This tree grows as large as the Pig-nut Hickery, and much like it in appearance. The nuts are ſmall, round, and thin ſhell'd, the kernel ſweet. The branches are ſlender and flexible. There is, I think, a variety of this, with a rougher furrowed bark, bearing broader leaves and larger nuts, having thicker

thicker outer covers, as well as inward ſhells, with the kernel generally ſmall and ſhrivelled. The timber of both kinds is hard and tough, and uſed for axle-trees of carriages, &c. mill coggs and rounds, and alſo for handles, &c. for moſt implements of huſbandry.

7. JUGLANS alba ovata. *Shell-barked Hickery.*

This tree delights in a rich moiſt ſoil, generally growing by creeks and rivers, often to the height of ſeventy or eighty feet, and above two feet in diameter. The bark is rough and ſhelly or ſcaly. The leaves are generally compoſed of two pair of lobes and an odd one, they are narrowed towards the baſe, oval, and pointed at the extremity, and ſawed on their edges. The fruit is roundiſh, but rather flatted and indented at the ends. The outer cover very thick and dividing into four parts, diſcloſing its nut, which is not very thick ſhell'd, containing ſweet kernel, preferable to the other kinds. There are ſeveral varieties of this in America, ſome with nuts as large as our common Walnuts.

8. JUGLANS pecan. *The Pecan, or Illinois Hickery.*

This tree is ſaid to grow plenty in the neighbourhood of the Illinois river, and other parts to the weſtward. The young plants raiſed from theſe nuts, much reſemble our young Pig-nut Hickerys. The nuts are ſmall and thin ſhelled.

JUNIPERUS.

The JUNIPER TREE.

Clafs 22. Order 12. Dioecia Monodelphia.

THE Flowers are *Male* and *Female* on different plants.
* The *Male*.
The *Calyx* is a conical katkin, confifting of a common rachis or ftring, to which three flowers are placed in triple oppofition, the katkin terminating with the tenth: each flower has for its bafe a *Scale* which is broad, fhort, incumbent and affixed to the column by a little footftalk.
The *Corolla* none.
The *Filaments* (in the terminal floret) are three, awl-fhaped, and joined beneath in one body; (in the lateral florets fcarce manifeft.) The *Antheræ* are three, diftinct in the terminal floret, but in the lateral joined to the fcales
* The *Female*.
The *Empalement* is three parted, very fmall, adjoining to the germen, and permanent.
The *Corolla* has three petals, permanent, rigid and acute.
The *Germen* is beneath. The *Styles* are three, fimple. The *Stigmas* are fimple.
The *Seed-veffel* is a berry, flefhy, roundifh, the under part marked with three obfolete oppofite tubercles, grown from the calyx, the top umbilicated with three fmall teeth (formerly petals.)
The *Seeds* are three, fmall, oblong, and bony, convex on one fide, and angled on the other.

The Species, *with us, are,*

1. JUNIPERUS virginiana. *Red Cedar-Tree.*

This tree often grows to the height of fifteen or twenty feet, fending off many diverging branches, covered with leaves fomething like the Juniper, but much fmaller, fhorter, and lying clofer to the branches. The berries are fmaller than thofe of the Juniper,

Juniper, and covered with a whitiſh ſubſtance, eaſily rubbing off.

2. JUNIPERUS caroliniana. *Red Carolinian Cedar.*

This tree much reſembles the former in ſize and ſhape, but the under leaves have ſomewhat the appearance of Juniper, the upper, of Cypreſs or Savin. There are ſaid to be other varieties, but their difference in appearance is ſcarcely obſervable. The timber affords very good durable poſts for fencing, &c.

KALMIA.

KALMIA, or AMERICAN LAUREL.

Claſs 10. Order 1. Decandria Monogynia.

THE *Empalement* is five parted, ſmall, and permanent: the ſegments are ſomewhat ovate, and acute.

The *Corolla* is of one petal, pitcher-funnel form. The *tube* is cylindrical and longer than the calyx. The *border* with a plane diſk, and erect half five cleft circumference; there are ten ſmall nectariferous horns, prominent without, and placed round the corolla from where the border is raiſed.

The *Filaments* are ten, awl-ſhaped, ſomewhat ſpreading, a little ſhorter than the corolla, and inſerted into its baſe. The *Antheræ* are ſimple.

The *Germen* is roundiſh. The *Style* is thread form, longer than the corolla, and declined. The *Stigma* is obtuſe.

The *Seed-veſſel* is roundiſh, depreſſed, five cell'd and five valv'd.

The *Seeds* are numerous.

The Species *are,*

1. KALMIA

1. KALMIA anguſtifolia. *Narrow leaved Kalmia.*

This kind delights in moiſt or ſwampy places, and riſes to the height of two feet or more. The leaves are of a light green colour, and ſometimes grow to the ſize of an inch and a half in length and half an inch in breadth, of an oval ſhape, and entire. The flowers come out in cluſters on every ſide of the ſtalks, towards their extremities, and are of a beautiful red colour. This has been called Glaucous leaved Kalmia.

2. KALMIA latifolia. *Broad leaved Kalmia.*

This beautiful flowering ſhrub riſes often to the height of ſix or eight feet and ſometimes to ten or twelve, covered with a lightiſh coloured rough bark, and generally growing crooked. The leaves are of a dark green colour, thick conſiſtence, lance-ſhaped and entire, in general about three inches in length and one in breadth. The flowers are produced in cluſters at the ends of the branches and are variegated with red when firſt opening, but change to a whiter colour when expanded. There are very few flowering ſhrubs comparable to this when in bloom. The leaves are noxious to oxen and ſheep, yet the deer eat them with impunity.

LAURUS.

The BAY-TREE.

Claſs 9. Order 1. Enneandria Monogynia.

THE *Empalement* is wanting.
The *Corolla* has ſix petals, ovate, ſharp pointed, concave, and erect: the alternate exterior.

And

And a *Nectarium*, conſiſting of three tubercles, ſharp pointed, coloured, and ending in two briſtles, ſtanding round the germen.

The *Filaments* are nine, ſhorter than the corolla, compreſſed, obtuſe and three-fold in each order. The *Antheræ* are adjoined on each ſide to the margin of the filaments.

There are two roundiſh ſmall *Glands* affixed by very ſhort footſtalks, to each filament of the inward order, near the baſe.

The *Germen* is ſomewhat ovate. The *Style* is ſimple, equal and the length of the ſtamina. The *Stigma* is obtuſe and oblique.

The *Seed-veſſel* is a drupe, oval, ſharp pointed, and one cell'd, contained in the calyx.

The *Seed* is a nut of a ſharp pointed egg-ſhape, with a kernel of the ſame form.

Obſ. The flowers are ſometimes male and female upon different trees.

The Species, *with us, are,*

1. LAURUS Benzoin. *The Benjamin-Tree, or Spice-Wood.*

This ſhrub grows naturally in moiſt places, and riſes often to the height of eight or ten feet, dividing into ſeveral branches. The leaves are annual, oval ſhaped and entire. The flowers are produced from the ſides of the branches upon ſhort footſtalks, often dividing and ſuſtaining from one, to four or five flowers, of a greeniſh yellow colour; which are ſucceeded by oval, oblong berries, of a red colour when ripe, but changing to black. The bark, berries, &c. have a ſtrong aromatic ſmell, much like that of Benzoin, and indeed, by ſome, is allowed to be the tree, from whence it is produced.

2. LAURUS Borbonia. *Red-ſtalked Carolinian Bay-Tree.*

This grows naturally in Carolina, and riſes with a ſtraight trunk to a conſiderable height, eſpecially near the ſea-coaſt. The leaves are ſharp pointed and much longer than thoſe of the European Bay; a little wooly underneath, veined tranſverſely, and ſomewhat reflexed on their edges. The male trees produce their flowers in long bunches from the wings of the leaves; the female, in looſe bunches, ſtanding upon long red footſtalks, and are ſucceeded by blue berries ſitting in red cups.

The wood is of a very fine grain, proper for cabinet making and other ornamental furniture. It alſo dies a beautiful black colour.

3. LAURUS geniculata. *Carolinian Spice Wood Tree.*

This kind ſo much reſembles the Benzoin as to require no further deſcription, except in having berries not of ſo red a colour.

4. LAURUS Saſſafras. *The Saſſafras-Tree.*

This tree riſes ſometimes to the height of twenty or thirty feet, and to twelve or fifteen inches in diameter, but is commonly of much lower growth. The bark of the young ſhoots is ſmooth and green, but of the old trunks rough, furrowed and of a lightiſh colour. It is divided towards the top into many branches, generally crooked, furniſhed with leaves different in form and ſize, ſome being oval and entire, others two or three lobed and of five or ſix inches in length, and nearly as much in width; of a light green colour and placed alternately upon pretty long footſtalks. The flowers are produced at the extremity of the former year's ſhoots upon long panicled footſtalks, and are generally male and female upon different trees. The female are ſucceeded by oblong, oval berries, of a bluiſh colour when ripe, ſitting in red cups, having red footſtalks. The roots and wood have been long uſed as a ſudorific, but the bark of the root is by much the ſtrongeſt, yielding a conſiderable quantity of hot, aromatic oil; and when powdered and joined with other febrifuges, has been given with ſucceſs in intermittents, &c. Alſo uſed as a tea, is ſaid to promote obſtructed menſes; but has been blamed for occaſioning the head-ach.

L E D U M.

MARSH CISTUS, or WILD ROSEMARY.

Claſs 10. Order 1. Decandria Monogynia.

THE *Empalement* is of one leaf, very ſmall, and five-toothed.

The *Corolla* conſiſts of five petals, ovate, concave, and ſpreading.

The *Filaments* are ten, thread-form, ſpreading and the length of the corolla. The *Antheræ* are oblong.

The *Germen* is roundiſh. The *Style* thread-form and the length of the ſtamina. The *Stigma* is obtuſe.

The *Seed-veſſel* is a capſule, roundiſh, five-cell'd and gaping in five parts at the top.

The *Seeds* are numerous, oblong, narrow, acute each way and very ſlender.

The Species *with us, but one,* viz.

LEDUM thymifolium. *Thyme leaved Marſh Ciſtus.*

This grows naturally in the Jerſeys, in low, moiſt places. It is a ſmall ever-green ſhrub, ſcarcely riſing above eighteen inches or two feet in height and divided into ſeveral branches. The leaves are very ſmall, entire, of an oblong oval ſhape, and thick conſiſtence,

consistence, placed close, alternately, and thick upon the branches. The flowers terminate the stalks in short leaffy bunches, coming out singly at the bosom of the leaves upon pretty long footstalks; they are small and white but make a fine appearance when in bloom. This has generally been called Thyme-leaved Kalmia.

LIQUIDAMBAR.

LIQUIDAMBAR, or SWEET GUM-TREE.

Class 21, Order 8. Monoecia Polyandria.

* THE *Male* Flowers are numerous in a conical, long, loose katkin.

The *Calyx* is a common Involucrum of four leaves; which are ovate, concave, and falling; the alternate shorter.

The *Corolla* none.

The *Filaments* are numerous, and very short, in a body, plane on one side and convex on the other. The *Antheræ* are erect, twin, four furrowed, and two cell'd.

* The *Female* flowers are collected in a globe at the base of the male spikes.

The *Calyx* is an Involucrum as in the male, but double.

The *Proper Empalement* is bell-shape, angled, warty, and many joined together.

The *Corolla* none.

The *Germen* is oblong and adjoined to the empalement. The *Styles* are two, awl-shaped. The *Stigmas* joined to these are the length of the style, recurved and downy.

The *Seed-vessel* consists of as many capsules as empalements, which are ovate, oblong, sharp pointed, with one cell and two valves at top; joined in a ligneous globe.

The *Seeds* are few, (one or two) oblong, pointed and shining; mixed with many branny corpuscles.

The Species *with us, are,*

1. LIQUIDAMBAR

1. LIQUIDAMBAR Styraciflua. *Maple-leaved Liquidambar-Tree, or Sweet Gum.*

This tree grows naturally in low clayey ground, riſing with a ſtraight trunk to the height of forty feet or more, ſending off many branches, forming a pyramidal head. The leaves are angular, ſomewhat reſembling thoſe of Maple, having five and often ſeven, pointed, ſerrated, ſpreading lobes; and are of a dark green colour. They have a ſtrong, ſweet, glutinous ſubſtance, exuding through their pores in warm weather, rendering them clammy to the touch. The flowers are produced early in the ſpring, and are ſucceeded by globular ſeed-veſſels, compoſed of many capſules joined at the baſe, but terminating in long ſoftiſh ſpines or points, and containing each one or two oblong compreſſed, winged ſeeds, with a great number of furfuraceous particles.

2. LIQUIDAMBAR aſplenifolia. *Spleen-wort-leaved Gale, or Shrubby Sweet Fern.*

This is a ſmall ſhrub, growing naturally upon dry ſlaty ridges, and ſeldom riſing above three feet high, dividing into ſeveral branches, furniſhed with many oblong leaves, alternately ſituated, reſembling thoſe of Spleen Wort; of a dark green colour, hairy underneath and ſitting cloſe to the ſtalks. The male katkins are produced lying cloſe to the ſmall branches near their ends. The female flowers are in ſmall heads a little beneath them, becoming ſmall burs, generally containing two or more oblong ſmooth ſeeds. An infuſion of the leaves has been uſed as an aſtringent in Diarrhœas, &c.

LIRIODENDRUM.

LIRIODENDRUM.

The TULIP-TREE.

Claſs 13. Order 7. Polyandria Polygynia.

THE *Calyx* conſiſts of a proper Involucrum of two leaves; which are triangular, plane and deciduous.

And an *Empalement* of three leaves; oblong, concave, ſpreading, petal-form, and deciduous.

The *Corolla* has ſix (often more) petals, bell'd: the petals are ſpatuled, oblong, obtuſe and variegated.

The *Filaments* are numerous, ſhorter than the corolla, linear, and inſerted in the receptacle. The *Antheræ* are linear, and adjoined longitudinally to the ſides of the filaments.

The *Germen* are numerous, placed in a cone. The *Style* none. The *Stigmas* globoſe.

The *Seed-veſſel* none. The ſeeds are imbricated in a cone like body.

The *Seeds* are numerous, ending in a lanced ſcale; near the baſe of the ſcale, ſending off from the interior ſide, an acute angle, compreſſed at the baſe and acute, by which they are joined to the ſpindle ſhaped receptacle.

The Species *with us, are,*

LIRIODENDRUM Tulipifera. *Virginian Tulip-Tree.*

This often grows to the ſize of a large tree, of ſeventy or eighty feet in height and above four feet in diameter. The bark of young trees is ſmooth, but as they grow old it becomes furrowed, their lower branches alſo falling off. The young trees ſend off many branches, almoſt from the ground upward, garniſhed with broad ſmooth leaves, heart-ſhaped at the baſe, but end-bitten, or cut, at the extremity, having two or three pointed lobes, on each ſide the midrib; of a dark green colour on the upper ſide,

ſide, but lighter and veined underneath; with pretty long footſtalks. The flowers are produced at the extremity of the branches in form of a Tulip, compoſed of ſix or ſeven petals, or ſometimes more, greeniſh coloured towards the tops, but marked tranſverſely with red, towards the claws; which are glandular and honey-bearing. The young trees make a beautiful appearance, eſpecially when in flower. We have two kinds of Tulip trees, *viz.* Yellow and White, their difference eaſily diſtinguiſhable by the wood or timber, but perhaps not otherwiſe. The Yellow is ſoft and brittle, and much uſed for boards, heels for ſhoes, &c. alſo turned into bowls, trenchers, &c. The white is heavy, tough, and hard, and likewiſe ſawed into joiſts, boards, &c. for building. The bark of the root is uſed as an ingredient in bitters, &c.

LONICERA.

HONEYSUCKLE, or WOODBINE.

Claſs 5. Order 1. Pentandria Monogynia.

THE *Empalement* is five parted, above and ſmall.
The *Corolla* is of one petal and tubulous. The *tube* oblong and gibboſe. The *border* five-parted; the diviſions revolute, and one deeper ſeparated than the reſt.
The *Filaments* are five, awl-ſhaped and nearly the length of the corolla. The *Antheræ* are oblong.
The *Germen* is roundiſh and beneath. The *Style* is thread-form and the length of the corolla. The *Stigma* is obtuſe-headed.
The *Seed-veſſel* is a berry, umbilicated and two cell'd.
The *Seeds* are roundiſh and compreſſed.

The Species, *with us, (according to* Linnæus'*s arrangement) are divided as follows, into*

* *Honeyſuckles*

* *Honeyſuckles with a trailing ſtalk.*

1. LONICERA caroliniana. *Carolinian ſcarlet Trumpet-flowered Honeyſuckle.*

This is a variety of the following, only differing in having ſmaller leaves and flowers.

2. LONICERA virginiana. *Virginian ſcarlet Honeyſuckle.*

This hath a ſhrubby trailing ſtalk, which requires ſupport, and appears much like the common Honeyſuckle, but the ſhoots are weaker. The inferior leaves are inverſe egg-ſhaped, of a deep green colour on their upper ſides, but whitiſh underneath, ſitting cloſe to the branches; but thoſe near the ends of the branches, are joined, forming ſometimes a large ſomewhat quadrangular leaf, but moſtly a ſmaller concave oval one. The flowers are produced in whorls upon a long naked ſtalk terminating the branches, having long ſcarlet tubes with ſhort borders. The lower leaves in warm ſituations are evergreen.

3. LONICERA ſempervirens. *Ever-green Honeyſuckle.*

This is ſaid to grow in Virginia, with ſtrong branches, covered with a purple bark, and garniſhed with lucid green leaves, continuing their verdure all the year. The flowers are produced in manner of the former, of a bright red on their outſides and yellow within, and continuing in ſucceſſion from June till autumn.

** *Dwarf*

** *Dwarf Cherries with biflorous footſtalks.*

4. LONICERA canadenſis. *Canadian dwarf-cherry Honeyſuckle.*

(Bartram's Catalogue.)

This is a native of Canada, riſing with an erect ſhrubby ſtalk to the height of about five feet. The leaves are oval ſhaped, entire, of a very thin texture and lucid green colour. The flowers terminate the branches, ſitting two upon each footſtalk, of a pale yellow colour, ſtreaked with purple, and appearing pretty early in the ſpring.

*** *With an erect ſtalk, and multiflorous footſtalks.*

5. LONICERA Diervilla. *Yellow flowering Diervilla.*

This hath ſlender ſhrubby ſtalks, ſeldom riſing above two feet and a half high, and generally leaning; furniſhed with ſomewhat heart-ſhaped, oblong, ſharp-pointed leaves, ſlightly ſawed on their edges, placed oppoſite, and ſitting cloſe to the ſtalks. The flowers are produced at the extremity and ſometimes from the ſides of the branches, generally two or three together, upon ſhort footſtalks; they are of a cream colour, the inferior ſegment of the flower ſomewhat larger and yellower than the others; they are ſucceeded by oblong capſules, containing ſmall ſeeds. This grows moſt natural upon mountains, and ſpreads much by its creeping roots.

6. LONICERA marylandica. *Maryland ſcarlet Lonicera.*

This, it is ſaid, grows in Maryland with an upright ſtalk, furniſhed with ovate, oblong, ſharp-

 pointed

pointed leaves, which are diſtinct and ſit cloſe to the ſtalks. The flowers are produced in erect ſpikes of a ſcarlet colour.

7. LONICERA Symphoricarpos. *Indian Currants, or St. Peter's Wort.*

This hath a ſhrubby ſtalk, which riſes from four to five feet high and ſpreads into many ſlender branches, garniſhed with oval entire leaves, ſomewhat hairy and placed oppoſite upon ſhort footſtallks. The flowers are ſmall and of an herbaceous colour, and are produced upon ſhort, common peduncles, or footſtalks, which are placed oppoſite a conderable diſtance along, and terminating the branches; upon which they are ſet very cloſe in whorls, or rather in two oppoſite rows. A few of theſe are ſucceeded by reddiſh, depreſſed, hollow and ſpongy berries; ripening very late, and each generally containing two ſmall round compreſſed ſeeds. This often ſends off a few weak trailing branches lying upon the ground and taking root, by which it may be eaſily propagated.

MAGNOLIA.

The LAUREL-LEAVED TULIP-TREE.

Claſs 13. Order 7. Polyandria Polygynia.

THE *Empalement* is three leaved: the leaves ovate, concave, petal form and deciduous.

The *Corolla* has nine petals, oblong, concave, obtuſe, and narrower at the baſe.

The *Filaments* are numerous, ſhort, ſharp pointed, and compreſſed; inſerted beneath the germen in the common receptacle of the ſtyles. The *Antheræ* are linear and adjoined on each ſide to the margin of the filaments.

The

The *Germen* are numerous, ovate-oblong, covering the clubbed receptacle. The *Styles* are recurved, contorted and very ſhort. The *Stigmas* are from one end of the ſtyle to the other, and villoſe.

The *Seed-veſſel* is an ovate cone, covered with *capſules*, which are compreſſed, roundiſh, ſcarce imbricated, crowded, acute, one cell'd, two valv'd, ſeſſile, gaping outward and permanent.

The *Seeds* are ſolitary, roundiſh, berried, and hanging by a thread from the boſom of each ſcale of the cone.

The Species *are,*

1. MAGNOLIA acuminata. *Long leaved Mountain Magnolia, or Cucumber Tree.*

This tree grows ſometimes to the height of thirty or forty feet, and to eighteen inches or more in diameter; dividing into ſeveral branches towards the top, garniſhed with large, oblong, ſharp-pointed leaves. The flowers come out early in the ſpring and are compoſed of twelve large bluiſh coloured petals. The ſeed-veſſels are about three inches long, ſomewhat reſembling a ſmall Cucumber; from whence the inhabitants where it grows natural, call it the Cucumber-tree.

2. MAGNOLIA glauca. *Small Magnolia, or Swamp Saſſafras.*

This grows naturally in low, moiſt, or ſwampy ground, often to the height of fifteen or twenty feet; covered with a whitiſh ſmooth bark, and dividing into ſeveral branches; furniſhed with entire, oblong, oval leaves, of a dark green on their upper ſurface, but whitiſh and a little hairy underneath. The flowers are produced at the ends of the branches, compoſed of ſix concave, white petals, of an agreeable ſmell; and are ſucceeded by oval, or ſomewhat conical ſeed-veſſels, of an inch or more in length and three fourths of an inch in diameter; compoſed of many capſules, which open and diſcharge their ſeeds when ripe, hanging by ſlender white threads, of a red colour, and near the ſize of a ſmall bean. The ſeeds and bark have been uſed with ſome ſucceſs in the cure of Rheumatiſm, &c.

3. MAGNOLIA grandiflora. *Ever-green Laurel-leaved Tulip-Tree.*

This grows naturally in Florida and South Carolina, ſometimes to the height of eighty feet or more, with a ſtraight trunk of two feet or more in diameter; having a regular head. The leaves are ever-green, of a thick conſiſtence, pretty large, oblong, pointed, and entire: of a lucid green on the upper ſide, and ſometimes of a ruſſet, or buff colour on the under. The flowers are produced at the ends of the branches; they are very large, and compoſed of eight or ten oblong white petals, narrowed towards the baſe, but broad, rounded, and a little waved at their extremities. They are ſucceeded by oblong, conical ſeed-veſſels, diſcloſing their ſeeds after the manner of the other ſpecies. This is allowed to be one of the moſt beautiful ever-green trees yet known, but is impatient of cold.

4. MAGNOLIA tripetala. *The Umbrella Tree.*

This grows pretty frequent in Carolina, and ſome parts of Pennſylvania; uſually to the height of ſixteen or twenty feet, with a ſlender trunk, covered with a ſmooth bark, and dividing into ſeveral branches. The leaves are very large and entire, often from twelve to fifteen inches or more in length, and five or ſix in width, narrowing to a point at each extremity,

placed

placed at the ends of the branches in a circular manner, ſomewhat reſembling an umbrella; from whence it obtained its name. The flowers are compoſed of ten, or eleven, large, oblong, white petals, the exterior ones hanging down; and are ſucceeded by oblong, conical ſeed-veſſels, between three and four inches in length, and about one and a half in diameter, growing reddiſh and diſcloſing their ſeeds, when ripe, after the ſame manner of the others. There are ſaid to be two other ſpecies in the ſouthern ſtates.

MENISPERMUM.

MOONSEED.

Claſs 22. Order 10. Dioecia Decandria.

THE Flowers are Male and Female upon ſeparate plants.
 * The *Male*.

The *Empalement* is two leaved: the leaves are linear and ſhort.

The *Corolla* has four *exterior* petals, which are ovate, ſpreading and equal. And eight *interior* leſſer ones, ovate and concave.

The *Filaments* are ſixteen (or more) cylindrical and rather longer than the corolla. The *Antheræ* are terminal, very ſhort, and obtuſe four lobed.

* The *Female*, on a different plant.

The *Empalement* as in the Male.

The *Corolla* as the Male.

The *Filaments* eight, like the male. The *Antheræ* are pellucid and barren.

The *Germen* are two, ovate, incurved, winking and pedicell'd. The *Styles* are ſolitary, very ſhort and recurved. The *Stigmas* are bifid and obtuſe.

The *Seed-veſſels* are two berries, roundiſh-kidney form and one cell'd.

The *Seeds* are ſolitary, large, and kidney form, or ſomewhat orbicular and compreſſed.

Obſ. The Canadian has an Empalement and Corolla of ſix leaves, alſo ſix ſtamina and three ſtyles.

The

The Species *with us, are,*

1. Menispermum canadenſe. *Canadian Moonſeed.*

This hath a thick, ligneous root, ſending up many twining ſtalks, twiſting themſelves round the neighbouring trees for ſupport, becoming woody, and riſing to the height of ten or fifteen feet. Theſe are furniſhed with large, ſmooth, roundiſh, angled leaves, having pretty long footſtalks placed on their under ſides, making a hollow, or appearance of a navel on the upper ſide. The flowers come out in looſe bunches from the ſides of the ſtalks; they are ſmall, of an herbaceous colour, and compoſed of ſix oblong petals, ſix ſhort ſtamina, and three ſtyles ariſing from as many germen; which become three channelled berries, each containing one ſomewhat circular compreſſed ſeed.

2. Menispermum carolinum. *Carolinian Moonſeed.*

This is much ſmaller and weaker than the other, ſcarcely becoming ſhrubby. The leaves are ſmaller, entire, heart-ſhaped, and villous underneath.

3. Menispermum virginicum. *Virginian Moonſeed.*

This much reſembles the Canadian kind, the leaves are target-form, heart-ſhaped and lobed.

MESPILUS.

MESPILUS.

The MEDLAR-TREE.

Claſs 12. Order 4. Icoſandria Pentagynia.

THE *Empalement* is one leaved, concave-ſpreading, five tooth-ed, and permanent.

The *Corolla* has five petals, roundiſh, concave, and inſerted in the calyx.

The *Filaments* are twenty, awl-ſhaped and inſerted in the calyx. The *Antheræ* are ſimple.

The *Germen* is beneath. The *Styles* are five, (often leſs) ſimple and erect. The *Stigmas* are headed.

The *Seed-veſſel* is a berry, globoſe, umbilicated, and covered with the calyx, but ſomewhat perforated at the apex.

The *Seeds* are five, bony and gibbous.

The Species, *with us, are,*

* *Armed with Thorns*

1. MESPILUS coccinea. *Cockſpur-Hawthorn.*

This riſes generally to the height of ten or twelve feet, with a pretty ſtrong ſtem, dividing into ſeveral branches, which are armed with ſtrong thorns, bent downwards like a cock's ſpur. The leaves are ſomewhat oval, but ſpreading into angles, ſawed on their edges, and ſmooth. The flowers come out at the extremities and ſides of the branches in umbels; they are pretty large and are ſucceeded by fruit nearly as large as a ſmall cherry and of a fine red colour when ripe.

There is a variety of this without thorns, with leaves deeper ſawed on their edges, and not ſo deeply veined, otherwiſe of the ſame growth and appearance.

2. MESPILUS Crus galli. *Pear leaved Thorn.*

This riſes with a ſtrong ſtem to the height of fifteen or twenty feet, ſending off many long (and often nearly horizontal) branches, armed with long, ſharp thorns. The leaves are of an oblong, oval ſhape, or often narrowed towards the baſe, ſawed on their edges, ſmooth, and of a deep, ſhining green colour, and thick conſiſtence. The flowers come out late, and are produced in ſmall cluſters at the ends of the branches. The fruit are of a middling ſize and of a dark or dirty reddiſh colour.

Obſ. The flowers have frequently but one ſtyle.

3. MESPILUS cuneiformis. *Wedge leaved Meſpilus.*

This grows often to the height of twenty feet or more, with a ſtrong ſtem of five or ſix inches in diameter, covered with a dark rough bark, dividing into many branches, and armed with long ſharp thorns. The leaves are ſmooth, wedge, or inverſe-egg-ſhaped, and pointed; ſlightly and ſomewhat doubly ſerrated towards their extremities, of a ſhining green colour on their upper ſurface and veined with oblique parallel veins. The flowers are produced in ſmall cluſters at the ends of the branches and are ſucceeded by middle ſized reddiſh fruit.

4. MESPILUS Azarolus major. *Great Azarole, or Hawthorn.*

This kind frequently riſes to the height of twelve or fifteen feet, with a ſtrong ſtem covered with a lightiſh rough bark, dividing into many branches, and armed with many long thorns. The leaves are

larger

larger than thofe of the other kinds, fomewhat egg-fhaped, but toothed or angled, fawed on their edges, and much veined. The flowers are produced in umbels at the extremity of the branches and are fucceeded by large fruit, of a dark red colour.

5. MESPILUS Azarolus minor. *Smaller Azarole, or Hawthorn.*

This has much the appearance of the laft, but is fmaller in growth, leaves and fruit.

6. MESPILUS Oxyacantha aurea. *Yellow berried Hawthorn.*

This rifes to the height of fix or eight feet, dividing into feveral branches and armed with fharp thorns. The leaves are fomewhat egg-fhaped, but acutely toothed and fawed on their edges. The flowers are produced as in the other kinds and are fucceeded by middling fized fruit, of a greenifh yellow colour when ripe.

7. MESPILUS apiifolia. *Virginian Parfley leaved Mefpilus.*

This is generally of low growth, rifing perhaps to the height of five or fix feet, and armed with a few fharp thorns. The leaves are fmall, fhining and much cut or divided on their edges. The fruit are fmall and red coloured.

** *Without Thorns.*

8. MESPILUS nivea. *Early ripe, Eſculent fruited Medlar, or wild Service.*

This riſes frequently to the height of fifteen or twenty feet, dividing into ſeveral branches, which are without thorns, and covered with a ſmooth, whitiſh, ſpotted bark. The leaves are of an oblong oval; pointed, ſlightly and acutely ſerrated, hairy and whitiſh at their firſt appearance, but becoming ſmooth and of a dark green, eſpecially upon their upper ſides. The flowers are produced from the ſides of the ſmall branches in looſe bunches or panicles, of a ſnowy white colour, and are ſucceeded by fruit near the ſize of a Gooſe-berry, which are ſoft, ſucculent, ſweet taſted, and purpliſh coloured when ripe. The flowers of this come out before the leaves are expanded, perfectly white, and thick ſet upon the branches, making a fine appearance. The fruit is ripe in June, pretty large and of an agreeable taſte. There is a variety of this of ſmaller growth, but of the ſame appearance.

9. MESPILUS prunifolia. *Plumb leaved Medlar.*

This grows naturally in moiſt places riſing with ſlender ſtems to the height of ſix or eight feet, dividing into but few branches and without thorns. The leaves are inverſe egg-ſhaped, pointed, ſlightly ſerrated, of a dark green on their upper ſurface, but lighter and downy underneath. The flowers are produced at the extremity of the branches in cluſters, and are ſucceeded by ſmall fruit of a dark purpliſh colour when ripe.

There is a variety of this, generally rising but to the height of two or three feet. The fruit are somewhat larger and of the same colour, but otherwise much resembling the other.

10. MESPILUS canadensis. *Dwarf red fruited Medlar.*

This rises to the height of four or five feet, with slender smooth stems, much resembling the last described, except in having fruit of a red colour when ripe. There is also a variety of this of smaller growth, which produces fruit of a beautiful red colour.

Obs. The characters of the Cratægus and Mespilus differ so immaterially that, I should suppose, they might be reduced to one Genus, with much greater propriety than the Beech and Chesnut. They are Genera in which much confusion prevails amongst Botanical writers, some classing most of the Species under the Cratægus, others the same Species under the Mespilus; neither is it easy to determine to which they, with most propriety, belong. I have frequently observed in some Species from one to three styles, in others from three to five, but not having observed any to be constant with two, agreeably to the character of the Cratægus, have ranged none under that Genus. We have, native of these states, several *Species* of Mespilus, and a great number of *Varieties*, which, until better discriminated and ascertained, can never be described with any degree of accuracy.

MITCHELLA.

MITCHELLA.

MITCHELLA.

Claſs 4. Order 1. Tetrandria Monogynia.

THE Flowers are twin, or two ſitting upon the ſame bud; and each having an *Empalement*, four parted, erect, permanent and above.

A *Corolla* of one petal, funnel form. The *tube* cylindrical; the *border* four-parted, ſpreading and hairy within.

And four *Filaments*, thread-form, erect, and within the boſom of the corolla. With *Antheræ* oblong, and acute.

The *Germen* is twin, orbiculate, common to both, and beneath. The *Styles* are one in each flower, thread-form and the length of the corolla. The *Stigmas* are four, oblong.

The *Seed-veſſel* is a berry, two parted and globoſe.

The *Seeds* are four, compreſſed and callous.

There is but one Species *of this Genus*, viz.

MITCHELLA repens. *Creeping evergreen Mitchella.*

This is a ſmall plant, growing upon moſſy, northern, ſhaded banks, with ſlender ſhrubby ſtalks, lying cloſe to the ground, and putting out roots at the joints. The leaves are ever-green, of a thick conſiſtence, obtuſely egg-ſhaped, and entire; they are placed oppoſite and thick upon the branches, with ſhort footſtalks, and are often marked longitudinally with a whitiſh vein. The flowers are produced at the boſom of the leaves, they are double, or two ariſing from one bud, of a white colour, and are ſucceeded by ſmall roundiſh red berries.

MORUS.

The MULBERRY-TREE.

Clafs 21. Order 4. Monoecia Tetrandria.

*THE *Male* Flowers are difpofed in Katkins.

The *Empalement* is four parted; the leaves ovate and concave.

The *Corolla* none.

The *Filaments* are four, awl-fhaped, erect, longer than the calyx, and one within each leaf of the flower cup. The *Antheræ* are fimple.

*The *Female* Flowers are collected, either in the fame, or a different plant from the male.

The *Empalement* is four leaved: the leaves are roundifh, obtufe, permanent; the two oppofite exterior incumbent.

The *Corolla* none.

The *Germen* is heart fhaped. The *Styles* are two, awl-fhaped, long, reflexed, and rough. The *Stigmas* are fimple.

The *Seed-veffel* none. The Empalements becoming flefhy fucculent berries, jointly forming an oblong rough fruit.

The *Seeds*, one in each berry, ovate acute.

We have but one Species, *native with us*, viz.

MORUS rubra. *Large-leaved Virginian Mulberry Tree.*

This grows common in many parts of North-America, to the height of twenty or thirty feet, and with a trunk from twelve to eighteen inches or more in diameter; dividing into many branches, which are garnifhed with large, rough, heart-fhaped, oblong, pointed leaves; fawed on their edges, and fometimes with others largely and deeply divided into two, three, or more pointed lobes. The leaves of male trees are generally largeft. The fruit is large, of a dark purplifh colour when ripe, very fucculent

culent and of an agreeable taſte. The timber affords very durable poſts, for fencing, &c. As our Mulberry has been found, upon trial, to anſwer well for the purpoſe of raiſing ſilk worms, and growing ſpontaneouſly and plentifully in many parts of theſe ſtates; it is preſumed, many of our countrymen might profitably apply their attention to the culture of ſilk.

MYRICA.

CANDLEBERRY MYRTLE.

Claſs 22. Order 5. Dioecia Tetrandria.

THE Flowers are *Male* and *Female* on different plants.

* The *Male*.

The *Calyx* is a Katkin ovate-oblong, looſe, imbricated on all ſides, and conſiſting of *Scales*, which are one flowered, moon-ſhape, obtuſely pointed, and concave.

The *Corolla* none.

The *Filaments* are four, (rarely ſix) thread-form, ſhort, and erect. The *Antheræ* are large and twin, with two-cleft lobes.

* The *Female*.

The *Calyx* and *Corolla* as in the male.

The *Germen* is ſomewhat ovate. The *Styles* are two, thread-form and longer than the calyx. The *Stigmas* are ſimple.

The *Seed-veſſel* is a berry, of one cell.

The *Seed* is one.

Obſ. The *Gale* has four ſtamina: the Berry compreſſed at the apex, and three lobed: the *cerifera* has ſix ſtamina: the berry ſucculent and roundiſh.

The Species *with us, are,*

1. MYRICA cerifera. *Candleberry Myrtle.*

This grows naturally upon low boggy lands, riſing with many ſtrong ſhrubby ſtalks, to the height of ſix or eight feet; ſending out ſeveral branches, which

which are furniſhed with ſtiff ſpear-ſhaped leaves, a little ſawed towards their extremities, of a yellowiſh lucid green on their upper ſides but paler underneath, having very ſhort footſtalks, and of a grateful odour when bruiſed. The katkins come out on different plants from the berries, and are about an inch long, ſtanding erect. The female flowers come out on the ſides of the branches in long bunches, and are ſucceeded by ſmall roundiſh berries, covered, with a mealy ſubſtance, and affording a kind of green wax, which is ſometimes uſed in making candles.

2. MYRICA cerifera humilis. *Dwarf Candleberry Myrtle.*

This is a variety of the former kind, differing from it in being of a lower growth, the branches not ſo ſtrong, and covered with a greyiſh bark. The leaves are alſo ſhorter and broader, and more ſawed on their edges. The berries afford a wax like the others.

3. MYRICA Gale. *American Bog Gale.*

This alſo grows naturally in bogs and ſwamps, riſing with ſhrubby ſtalks to the height of two or three feet, garniſhed with lance-ſhaped leaves, ſmooth and a little ſawed towards their points. The berries are dry, compreſſed at the apex and three lobed.

NYSSA.

The TUPELO-TREE.

Claſs 23. Order 1. Polygamia Dioecia.

THE Flowers are *Male* and *Hermaphrodite*, (in ſome Species *Male* and *Female*) upon different plants.

* The

* The *Male*.

The *Empalement* is five-parted and ſpreading, with a plane bottom.

The *Corolla* none.

The *Filaments* are ten, awl-ſhaped and ſhorter than the calyx. The *Antheræ* are twin and the length of the filaments.

* The *Hermaphrodite*.

The *Empalement* as in the male, ſitting upon the germen.

The *Corolla* none.

The *Filaments* are five, awl-ſhaped, and erect. The *Antheræ* are ſimple.

The *Germen* is ovate and beneath. The *Style* is awl-ſhaped, incurved, and longer than the ſtamina. The *Stigma* is acute.

The *Seed-veſſel* is a drupe, ovate and one cell'd.

The *Seed* is a nut, oval, acute, hollowed with longitudinal furrows, angled, and irregular.

Obſ. The Nyſſa ſylvatica is Male and Female on different trees.

The Species *are*,

1. NYSSA aquatica. *Virginian Water Tupelo-Tree.*

This grows naturally in wet ſwamps, or near large rivers, in Carolina and Florida; riſing with a ſtrong upright trunk to the height of eighty or an hundred feet, dividing into many branches towards the top. The leaves are pretty large, of an oval, ſpear-ſhaped form, generally entire, but ſometimes ſomewhat toothed, and covered underneath with a whitiſh down: they are joined to long, ſlender footſtalks, and affixed to the branches in ſomewhat of a verticillate order, preſenting a beautiful varied foliage. The berries are near the ſize and ſhape of ſmall olives, and are preſerved in like manner by the French inhabitants upon the Miſſiſſippi, where it greatly abounds, and is called the Olive tree. The timber is white and ſoft when unſeaſoned, but light and

and compact when dry, which renders it very proper for making trays, bowls, &c.

2. NYSSA Ogeche. *The Ogeche Lime Tree.*

(Bartram's Catalogue.)

This is a tree of great ſingularity and beauty; growing naturally in water, in the ſouthern ſtates, and riſing to the height of about thirty feet. The leaves are oblong, of a deep ſhining green on their upper ſides, and lightly hoary underneath. The flowers are male and female upon different trees, and are produced upon divided, or many flowered footſtalks. The fruit is nearly oval, of a deep red colour, of the ſize of a Damaſcene Plumb, and of an agreeable acid taſte; from which it is called the Lime-tree. Perhaps this is the *multiflora* of Weſton.

3. NYSSA ſylvatica. *Upland Tupelo-Tree, or Sour Gum.*

This grows naturally in Pennſylvania and perhaps elſewhere, riſing with a ſtrong upright trunk to the height of thirty or forty feet, and ſometimes of near two feet in diameter; ſending off many horizontal, and often depending branches; garniſhed with oval, or rather inverſe egg-ſhaped leaves, a little pointed, entire, of a dark green and ſhining upper ſurface, but lighter and a little hairy underneath: thoſe of male trees are often narrower and ſometimes lance-ſhaped. The flowers are produced upon pretty long common footſtalks, ariſing from the baſe of the young ſhoots, and dividing irregularly into ſeveral parts, generally from ſix to ten; each ſupporting a ſmall flower, having an empalement of ſix or ſeven linear, unequal leaves, and from ſix to eight awl-ſhaped ſpreading ſtamina, ſupporting ſhort four lobed Antheræ. The female trees have fewer flowers produced upon much longer, ſimple, cylindrical footſtalks, thickened at the extremity, and ſupporting generally three flowers, ſitting cloſe and having a ſmall involucrum. They are compoſed of five ſmall oval leaves, and in the center an awl-ſhaped incurved ſtyle, ariſing from the oblong germen, which is beneath, and becomes an oval oblong berry, of a dark purpliſh colour when ripe. The timber of this tree is cloſe grained and curled ſo as not to be ſplit or parted; and therefore much uſed for hubs of wheels for waggons, carriages, &c.

O L E A.

The O L I V E - T R E E.

Claſs 2. Order 1. Diandria Monogynia.

THE *Empalement* is of one leaf, tubular, and ſmall: the border four-toothed, erect and deciduous.

The *Corolla* is one petal'd, funnel-form. The tube cylindrical, the length of the empalement. The border four-parted and plain: the diviſions ſemi-ovate.

The *Filaments* two, oppoſite, awl-ſhaped and ſhort. The *Antheræ* erect.

The *Germen* is roundiſh. The *Style* ſimple, very ſhort. The *Stigmas* two-cleft, thickened, the diviſions end-nicked.

The *Seed-veſſel* a *drupe*, ſomewhat ovate, ſmooth, and one cell'd.

The *Seed* ovate-oblong, and wrinkled,

The Species *with us*,

OLEA americana. *American Olive Tree.*

This grows naturally in Carolina and Florida, and is a beautiful ever-green tree. The leaves are nearly ovate, or ſomewhat oblong, perennial, of a ſhining, full

full green, on their upper ſurface, and of a ſolid conſiſtence. The fruit or berries are nearly oval, of the ſize of a ſparrow's egg, of a beautiful bluiſh purple, and covered with a nebula or gloom.

PHILADELPHUS.

SYRINGA, or MOCK-ORANGE.

Claſs 12. Order 1. Icoſandria Monogynia.

THE *Empalement* is one leaved, four parted, ſharp pointed, and permanent.

The *Corolla* has four petals, roundiſh, plane, large and ſpreading.

The *Filaments* are twenty, awl-ſhaped and the length of the calyx. The *Antheræ* are erect and four furrowed.

The *Germen* is beneath. The *Style* is thread form and four-parted. The *Stigmas* are ſimple.

The *Seed-veſſel* is a capſule, oval, ſharp-pointed, part ſurrounded by the calyx, with four cells, and four valves.

The *Seeds* are numerous, oblong and ſmall.

We have, with us, but one Species, viz.

PHILADELPHUS inodorus. *Carolinian Scentleſs Syringa.*

This is ſaid to grow naturally in Carolina; riſing with a ſhrubby ſtalk to the height of twelve or fifteen feet, ſending out oppoſite branches, furniſhed with ſmooth, entire leaves, ſhaped like thoſe of the Pear tree, but ſtanding oppoſite upon pretty long footſtalks. The flowers are pretty large and have large empalements of four acute-pointed leaves, and four white, oval, ſpreading petals, and a great number of ſtamina with yellow ſummits. This is impatient of much cold.

PINUS.

PINUS.

The PINE-TREE.

Claſs 21. Order 9. Monoecia Polyandria.

* THE *Male* Flowers are diſpoſed in Racemi or bunches.
The *Calyx* none but the ſcales of the bud, gaping.
The *Corolla* none.
The *Filaments* are numerous and joined beneath in an erect column, divided at top. The *Antheræ* are erect.
* The *Female* Flowers are in the ſame plant.
The *Calyx* is a common, ſomewhat ovate cone, conſiſting of *Scales*, which are two flowered, oblong, imbricated, rigid, and permanent.
The *Corolla* none.
The *Germen* is very ſmall. The *Style* is awl-ſhaped. The *Stigma* ſimple.
The *Seed-veſſel* none, but the ſcales of the cone.
The *Seed* is a nut, increaſed with a membranaceous wing, which is larger than the ſeed, but ſmaller than the ſcale of the cone, oblong, ſtraight on one ſide and gibbous on the other.

The Species, *with us*, *are*,

1. PINUS echinata. *Three leaved prickly-coned Baſtard Pine.*

This grows naturally in Virginia. The leaves are long and narrow, ſometimes three, at other times but two in each ſheath. The cones are long and ſlender, their ſcales terminating in ſharp points.

2. PINUS paluſtris. *Longeſt three leaved Marſh Pine.*

This grows naturally in South Carolina, and is of a middling growth. The leaves are produced by threes in a ſheath and are often ten or twelve inches in in length. The cones are long and large, opening and dropping their ſeeds in the fall. It is accounted equal to any for yielding tar, &c.

3. PINUS rigida. *Common three leaved Virginian Pine.*

This grows common in many places throughout theſe ſtates, riſing often to the height of ſixty or ſeventy feet, with a large erect trunk, dividing into branches towards the top, and furniſhed with pretty long leaves growing by threes in a ſheath. The cones are often produced in cluſters round the branches. they are about three inches long and have rigid ſcales. There are whole Foreſts of many hundred acres of theſe trees in ſome back parts of the country, of which great quantities of Boards are ſawed and floated down ſome of our long rivers.

4. PINUS Strobus. *New-England, or White Pine.*

This is allowed to out top in growth moſt of our other trees, riſing with a large erect trunk, to the height of an hundred feet or more, covered with a ſmooth bark and ſending off many long branches. The leaves are long and ſlender, growing by fives in a ſheath, and ſet thick on the branches. The cones are often ſix or ſeven inches in length, and generally beſmeared with turpentine, with which theſe trees much abound. The cones generally open about the firſt of September, ſoon after which the ſeeds drop out. This alſo grows in great plenty towards the heads of ſome of our rivers, from whence great quantities are rafted down, affording excellent maſts, yards, ſpars, &c. &c. for ſhip building.

5. PINUS

5. PINUS Tæda. *Virginian Swamp, or Frankincence Pine.*

This grows to a pretty large ſize, the leaves are very long and narrow and are produced by threes in a ſheath. The cones are pretty long and large. This is uſeful for boards, and for producing turpentine and tar, as are the other kinds.

6. PINUS virginiana. *Two-leaved Virginian, or Jerſey Pine.*

This is generally of but low growth, but divided into many branches. The leaves are broader and ſhorter than the other kinds, and of a deeper green colour; they are produced by twos in each ſheath. The cones are ſmall, each ſcale terminating with a prickly point. This is called, in ſome places, Spruce Pine.

PINUS-ABIES.

The FIR-TREE.

1. PINUS-ABIES Balſamea. *Balm of Gilead Fir-Tree.*

This tree grows to the height of thirty or forty feet, ſending off many branches, which are thick ſet chiefly upon two ſides, with ſtiff linear leaves, reſembling thoſe of the Yew. The ſurface of the trunk is almoſt covered with ſmall bladders, or riſings in the cuticle of the bark, which are filled with a clear balſam or turpentine. The cones are pretty large, and fall to pieces in the autumn.

2. PINUS-ABIES canadenſis. *Newfoundland Spruce.*

There are ſaid to be three varieties of this, diſtinguiſhed by the colour of their cones, into white, red and black; ſome of which, ſometimes become pretty large trees. The leaves are ſtiff and linear, and ſlightly channelled on both ſides, ſmaller than thoſe of the Balm of Gilead, and ſet equally upon all ſides of the branches. The trees make a very good appearance, and of theſe the famous Spruce-beer is brewed.

3. PINUS-ABIES americana. *Hemlock Spruce Fir-Tree.*

This riſes up with but a ſlender trunk, ſometimes to a great height, and is generally thick ſet with ſomewhat horizontal branches. The leaves are ſhaped much like thoſe of the Yew and are ranged upon two ſides of the branches, ſo appearing flat, like thoſe of the European Silver Firs, but are of a pale green on both ſides. The cones are very ſmall, looſe, and of an oval oblong form. The bark is ſaid to be good for tanning leather; and with it, our natives dye their ſplints for baſkets of a red colour.

PINUS-LARIX.

The LARCH-TREE.

1. PINUS-LARIX rubra. *Red American Larch-Tree.*

This ſhoots up to a conſiderable height with a ſlender erect trunk, ſending off many ſlender branches. The

The leaves are pretty long, linear and ſoft, coming out in faſciculi, or ſmall bundles ſpreading like a painter's bruſh, and are ſet pretty thick round the branches. They are of a light green colour and deciduous. The cones are of a fine red colour at their firſt appearance; they are ſmall, perhaps three-fourths of an inch long, and half an inch thick, the ſcales ſmooth, opening early in the fall and dropping their ſeeds, which are very ſmall and winged.

2. Pinus-Larix alba. *White American Larch-Tree.*

This a variety of the other, differing very little, except in the cones, being of a greeniſh white colour.

3. Pinus-Larix nigra. *Black American Larch-Tree.*

This is alſo a variety differing in having dark coloured cones.

PLATANUS.

The PLANE-TREE.

Claſs 21. Order 8. Monoecia Polyandria.

THE Flowers are *Male* and *Female* upon the ſame plant.
* The *Male* Flowers are diſpoſed in a globoſe katkin.
The *Calyx* conſiſts of ſome very ſmall ſegments.
The *Corolla* is ſcarce manifeſt.
The *Filaments* are oblong, thicker above, and coloured. The *Antheræ* are four cornered, moving round the filaments to the inferior ſide.
* The *Female* Flowers are diſpoſed in a globe.
The *Calyx* conſiſts of many ſmall ſcales.
The *Corolla* of many petals, concave, oblong and clubbed.

The

The *Germen* are many, diſpoſed in a globe and ending in awl-ſhaped *Styles*, with recurved *Stigmas*.
The *Seed-veſſel* none. But a globoſe receptacle.
The *Seeds* are oblong, angular and clubbed, crowned by the permanent ſtyle, and with a capillary pappus adhering at the baſe.
Obſ. I am in doubt with regard to the petals.

We have, with us, but one Species, *viz.*

PLATANUS occidentalis. *American Plane-Tree, or Large Button Wood.*

This grows common by creeks and river ſides in many parts of America. It is of quick growth, and often becomes a large tree of ſixty or ſeventy feet in height and above three feet in diameter, ſending off but few long, diverging branches, which together with the upper part of the trunk, are generally covered with a ſmoothiſh bark, annually, or often renewed, and falling off in thin plates or ſcales. The leaves are broad, and cut into angles, or lobed; having ſeveral acute indentures on their borders, of a light green on their upper ſide, but paler, and a little wooly underneath; with long footſtalks, and placed alternately. The flowers are produced in round pendulous balls, of near an inch in diameter, upon very long footſtalks. This is ſometimes ſawed into boards, and has been much uſed of late by our card-makers, for card-boards or backs.

POPULUS.

The POPLAR-TREE,

Claſs 22. Order 7. Dioecia Octandria.

THE Flowers are *Male* and *Female* on different Plants.
* The *Male*.

The *Calyx* is a common katkin, oblong, loofely imbricated, and cylindrical; compofed of *Scales* which are one flowered, oblong, and plane, with the margin torn.

The *Corolla* none, but

A *Nectarium* of one leaf, top fhaped and tubulous beneath, but oblique and terminating in an oval border above.

The *Filaments* are eight, very fhort. The *Antheræ* are four-cornered and large.

* The *Female*.

The *Katkin*, *Scales*, and *Nectaria*, are like the Male.

The *Germen* is ovate-fharp pointed. The *Style* is fcarce manifeft The *Stigma* is four cleft.

The *Seed-veffels* are ovate capfules, two-cell'd and two valv'd: the valves reflexed.

The *Seeds* are numerous and ovate, with a volatile capillary pappus.

The Species, *with us, are,*

1. POPULUS deltoide. *White Poplar, or Cotton Tree of Carolina.*

(Bartram's Catalogue.)

This becomes a tall tree, with a large erect trunk, covered with a white, fmoothifh bark, refembling that of the Afpen tree. The leaves are large, generally nearly triangular, toothed or indented with fharp and deep ferratures, of a fhining full green on their upper furface, but fomewhat lighter or hoary underneath; ftanding upon long flender footftalks, and generally reftlefs or in motion. The timber is white, firm, and elaftic, principally ufed for fence rails. It grows naturally upon rich low lands, on the banks of large rivers in Carolina and Florida.

2. POPULUS

2. POPULUS heterophylla. *Virginian Poplar-Tree.*

This becomes a pretty large tree, the branches of which are nerved, appearing as if quadrangular. The leaves are large and varioufly fhaped, fome roundifh, others heart-form, flightly fawed on their edges and downy at their firft appearance.

3. POPULUS nigra. *Black Poplar.*

This is not of very large growth, but covered with a darkifh rough bark. The leaves are fomewhat triangular, pretty long pointed, flightly and obtufely fawed on their edges, ftanding upon pretty long footftalks, fmooth and of a bright green on their upper furface, but lighter and a little downy underneath.

4. POPULUS tremula. *American Afpen-Tree.*

This grows frequently to the height of about thirty feet, covered with a fmooth whitifh bark. The leaves are fmall, fmooth on both fides, of a dark green colour above, but lighter underneath; roundifh, and a little pointed, or forming nearly an equilateral fpherical triangle; flighty crenated, a little waved on their edges, and trimmed with a very narrow hairy border. Their footftalks are pretty long, roundifh at the bafe, but compreffed on their fides towards the bafe of the leaves. The katkins are large appearing early in the fpring.

5. POPULUS balfamifera. *Balfam, or Tacamahac-Tree.*

This is a tree of but middling growth, covered with a light brown bark. The leaves are large, fomewhat ſomewhat heart-ſhaped, lightly toothed, or crenated on their edges, of a dark green on their upper ſurface but lighter underneath. The buds abound with a glutinous reſin, which is the tacamahacca of the ſhops.

6. POPULUS balſamifera lanceolata. *Lance-leaved Balſam Tree.*

This is a variety of the laſt kind, of a ſmall and very ſlow growth. The leaves are ſpear-ſhape, of a bright green above, but whitiſh and variegated with browniſh veins beneath, with a few, ſcarce obſervable, ſerratures on their edges, and joined to ſhort, channelled, and often ſomewhat reddiſh footſtalks.

POTENTILLA.

SHRUB CINQUEFOIL.

Claſs 12. Order 5. Icoſandria Polygynia.

THE *Empalement* is of one leaf, planiſh, and half five cleft: the alternate diviſions are leſs and reflexed.

The *Corolla* has five petals, roundiſh, ſpreading, and inſerted by claws in the calyx.

The *Filaments* are twenty, awl-ſhaped, ſhorter than the corolla, and inſerted in the calyx. The *Antheræ* are elongate-moon-ſhaped.

The *Germen* are numerous, very ſmall and collected in a little head. The *Styles* are thread-form, the length of the ſtamina, and inſerted in the ſides of the germen. The *Stigmas* are obtuſe.

The *Seed-veſſel* none, but a common receptacle, which is roundiſh, juiceleſs, very ſmall, permanent, covered with ſeeds and included in the calyx.

The *Seeds* are numerous and ſharp pointed.

We have but one Species, viz.

POTEN-

POTENTILLA fruticoſa americana. *American ſhrubby Cinquefoil.*

This is a ſmall ſhrub, ſeldom riſing above two feet high, and ſpreading into many branches. The leaves are ſmall and thick ſet upon the branches, they are winged, and compoſed, generally, of five ſmall, oblong hairy lobes, reflexed on their edges and ſtanding together. The flowers are produced pretty thick on the branches, of a yellow colour, and are ſucceeded by ſmall heads of pointed ſeeds.

PRINOS.

The WINTER-BERRY.

Claſs 6. Order 1. Hexandria Monogynia.

THE *Empalement* is one leaved, plane, half-ſix-cleft, very ſmall, and permanent.

The *Corolla* has one petal, wheel-ſhaped. The *tube* none. The *border* is ſix parted and plane: the diviſions ovate.

The *Filaments* are ſix, awl-ſhaped, erect and ſhorter than the corolla. The *Antheræ* are oblong and obtuſe.

The *Germen* is ovate, ending in a *Style* ſhorter than the ſtamina, with an obtuſe *Stigma*.

The *Seed-veſſel* is a roundiſh berry, with ſix cells; and far larger than the calyx.

The *Seeds* are ſolitary, bony, obtuſe, convex on one ſide and angled on the other.

Obſ. Sometimes a ſixth part of the number is excluded.

There are two Species *of this Shrub*, viz.

1. PRINOS glaber. *Evergreen Winter-Berry.*

This grows in ſeveral parts of North America, riſing up with ſlender ſhrubby ſtalks to the height of ſix or eight feet, dividing into branches, which are garniſhed garnifhed with fmall, evergreen, oblong, fmooth leaves, of a thick confiftence, with a few flight ferratures towards their points, and placed alternate, upon fhortifh footftalks. The flowers are produced from the bofom of the leaves upon fhort footftalks; and are fucceeded by fmall roundifh berries, of a black colour when ripe.

2. PRINOS verticillatus. *Virginian Winter-Berry.*

This grows naturally in moift places, by ftreams of water; generally fending up feveral flender ftalks to the height of eight or ten feet, dividing into a few branches towards the top. The leaves are lance-fhaped, fharp pointed, and acutely fawed on their edges; having fhort flender footftalks, and placed alternately. The flowers come out at the bofom of the leaves in fmall Corymbi or Clufters; of an herbaceous colour. They are fucceeded by roundifh berries of a red colour when ripe, and remaining long on the branches, almoft furrounding them in places and fomewhat refembling a whorl.

Note, The inner bark of this fhrub is very good to make poultices of for ripening tumors.

PRUNUS.

The PLUMB-TREE.

Clafs 12. Order 1. Icofandria Monogynia.

THE *Empalement* is one leaved, bell-fhaped, five cleft, and deciduous; the divifions are obtufe and concave.

The *Corolla* has five petals, roundifh, concave, large, fpreading, and inferted by claws in the calyx.

The *Filaments* are from twenty to thirty, awl-fhaped, near the length of the corolla, and inferted in the calyx. The *Antheræ* are twin and fhort.

The

The *Germen* is roundiſh. The *Style* is thread-form and the length of the ſtamina. The *Stigma* is orbiculate.
The *Seed-veſſel* is a roundiſh drupe.
The *Seed* is a nut, roundiſh and compreſſed.

The Species, *with us, are,*

1. PRUNUS americana. *Large Yellow Sweet Plumb.*

This generally riſes to the height of twelve or fifteen feet, ſpreading into many ſtiff branches. The leaves are oblong, oval, acute pointed, ſharply ſawed on their edges and much veined. The flowers generally come out very thick round the branches, often upon thick ſhort ſpurs; and are ſucceeded by large oval fruit, with a ſweet ſucculent pulp. We have a great variety of theſe, growing naturally in a good, moiſt ſoil, with reddiſh and yellowiſh fruit, but differing much in ſize, taſte, and conſiſtence.

2. PRUNUS anguſtifolia. *Chicaſaw Plumb.*

This is ſcarcely of ſo large a growth as the former, but riſing with a ſtiff ſhrubby ſtalk, dividing into many branches, which are garniſhed with ſmooth lance-ſhaped leaves, much ſmaller and narrower than the firſt kind; a little waved on their edges, marked with very fine, ſlight, coloured ſerratures, and of an equal, ſhining green colour, on both ſides. The bloſſoms generally come out very thick, and are ſucceeded by oval, or often ſomewhat egg-ſhaped fruit, with a very thin ſkin, and ſoft ſweet pulp. There are varieties of this with yellow and crimſon coloured fruit. Theſe being natives of the ſouthern ſtates, are ſomewhat impatient of much cold.

3. PRUNUS miſſiſſippi. *Crimſon Plumb.*

This grows naturally upon the Miſſiſſippi, and is of larger ſize than moſt of the other kinds. The fruit are crimſon coloured, and ſomewhat acid.

4. PRUNUS maritima. *Sea ſide Plumb.*

This grows naturally towards the ſea coaſt, riſing to the height of eight or ten feet, often leaning, and ſpreading into many branches. The leaves are oblong, rather ſmaller and not ſo pointed as thoſe of the common plumb; ſmooth and of a ſhining green on the upper ſide, but ſomething lighter underneath, and ſlightly ſawed on the edges. This is generally well filled with flowers, a few of which are ſucceeded by ſmall, roundiſh fruit.

5. PRUNUS declinata. *Dwarf Plumb.*

This is of a ſmall dwarfiſh growth, ſeldom riſing above four or five feet high, but frequently bearing fruit at the height of two or three; which is ſmall, and almoſt black when ripe.

To this Genus *alſo belongs*

CERASUS.

The CHERRY-TREE.

Of which our Species *are,*

1. PRUNUS-CERASUS virginiana. *Virginian Bird-Cherry-Tree.*

This grows naturally in a rich moiſt ſoil, often to the height of forty feet or more, with a trunk of eighteen

eighteen or twenty inches in diameter, generally retaining its thicknefs a confiderable height, and branching out towards the top. The leaves are lance-fhaped, or long, narrow, pointed, and fawed on their edges. The flowers are produced in bunches, generally pretty thick fet on the branches; they are of a white colour, and are fucceeded by fmall fruit, of a purplifh colour when ripe, and of a difagreeable, bitter tafte, but greedily devoured by the birds.

The timber is of a reddifh ftreaked colour, capable of receiving a fine polifh; and is frequently fawed into boards, and ufed by joiners, cabinent-makers, &c. for many purpofes.

2. PRUNUS-CERASUS canadenfis. *Canadian, or Dwarf Bird-Cherry-Tree.*

This is a fmall kind, growing to the height of fix or eight feet, and dividing into branches, which are furnifhed with broader and fhorter leaves, fomewhat refembling thofe of the Apple, or Crab-tree, but fmaller. The flowers are produced in a racemus, or bunch, compofed of more footftalks than the Virginian kind; and are fucceeded by fruit of near the fame colour and fize, not of fo bitter a tafte, but greatly corrugating the mouth and throat, fo as to obtain the name of Choak-Cherry.

3. PRUNUS-CERASUS montana. *Mountain Bird-Cherry-Tree.*

This grows naturally upon the mountains in the back parts of Pennfylvania; rifing up with a flender ftem to the height of twelve or fifteen feet, and dividing into a few very flender branches, furnifhed with leaves refembling the firft, or Virginian kind.

The fruit is likewiſe produced in the ſame manner, but is ſmaller, of a red colour, and an extremely acid taſte.

And alſo to the Genus Prunus, *belongs*,

LAURO-CERASUS.

The LAUREL-TREE.

Of which we have but one Species, viz.

PRUNUS-LAURO-CERASUS ſerratifolia. *Carolinian Evergreen Bay-tree.*

This is a beautiful evergreen ſhrub, but of ſmall growth; ſpreading with lateral branches, on every ſide and covered with a brown bark. The leaves are ſpear-ſhaped, above two inches long and three quarters of an inch or more in breadth, with a few ſharp ſerratures on their edges, ſtanding alternately on very ſhort footſtalks, of a thick conſiſtence, and ſhining green colour, continuing their verdure all the year. The flowers are generally very numerous, perfectly white, and are ſucceeded by roundiſh fruit of the ſize of a middling cherry, of a black colour when ripe. This is a native of South Carolina, and other ſouthern States.

PTELEA.

PTELEA.

Claſs 4. Order 1. Tetrandria Monogynia.

THE *Empalement* is five-parted, acute, and ſmall.

The *Corolla* has four petals, ovate-lanced, plane, ſpreading, larger than the calyx, and coriaceous.

The

The *Filaments* are four, awl-shaped. The *Antheræ* are roundish.
The *Germen* is orbiculate and compressed. The *Style* is short.
The *Stigmas* are two, a little obtuse.
The *Seed-vessel* is a roundish, perpendicular membrane, in the center two cell'd.
The *Seed* is one, obtuse, and lessened at the base.
Obs. The Petals and stamina, also the divisions of the calyx, have often one added to their number.

We have, with us, but one Species, viz.

PTELEA trifoliata. *Carolinian Shrub-Trefoil.*

This rises with an upright woody stem, to the height of ten or twelve feet, dividing into many branches, covered with a smooth greyish bark. The leaves are trifoliate, or composed of three oval, spear-shaped lobes, of a bright green on their upper side, but paler underneath, and inserted together at the end of a pretty long footstalk. The flowers terminate the branches in a kind of umbel, or large branching heads, of a whitish herbaceous colour; and are succeeded by roundish, flat, bordered capsules, somewhat resembling those of the Elm, each containing two seeds.

PYROLA.

WINTER-GREEN.

Class 10. Order 1. Decandria Monogynia.

THE *Empalement* is five-parted, small, and permanent.
The *Corolla* is composed of five petals, which are roundish, concave, and spreading.
The *Filaments* are ten, awl-shaped, shorter than the corolla.
The *Antheræ* are nodding, large, and two-horned upward.
The *Pistillum* has a roundish, angular *Germen*; a filiform, permanent *Style*, longer than the stamina; and a thickish *Stigma*.

The

The *Pericarpium*, or *Seed-veſſel*, is a roundiſh, depreſſed, pentagonal *Capſule*, with five cells, gaping at the angles.
The *Seeds* are numerous and chaffy.
Obſ. The Stamina and ſtyle differ ſometimes in ſituation.

The Species, *with us, are,*

1. PYROLA maculata. *Spotted Pyrola.*

This is a ſmall plant, ſeldom riſing above four or five inches high, with ſlender ligneous ſtalks. The leaves are ever-green, oblong and pointed, of a thick conſiſtence, with a few ſharp ſerratures on their edges; ſmooth and of a dark green on their upper ſides, but marked with a broad, branching, longitudinal vein or ſtreak, of a whitiſh or paler colour; and ſomewhat reddiſh underneath. There are generally three or four of theſe placed at the top of the ſtem ſomewhat horizontally, and ſometimes ſmaller ones beneath, ſet by threes. The flowers are likewiſe produced at the top upon a pretty long, (nodding at firſt, but afterwards erect) divided footſtalk, often ſuſtaining two or three white flowers, which are ſucceeded by roundiſh, depreſſed capſules, filled with ſmall ſeeds.

2. PYROLA rotundifolia. *Round leaved Pyrola.*

This is of ſmaller growth than the former, having about three or four roundiſh leaves, riſing from the root, with pretty long three ſided footſtalks, channelled above. Theſe often become pretty large and a little waved on their edges, they are of a light green, and ſcarcely perennial. The flowers are produced upon a radical triangular footſtalk, of four or five inches in length, in form of a racemus or bunch, ſupporting five or ſix white flowers, which are ſucceeded by ſmall, round, depreſſed capſules.

3. PYROLA umbellata. *Umbellated Pyrola.*

This grows commonly to the height of five or ſix inches, generally ſet pretty thick with leaves, which are wedge-ſhaped or narroweſt towards the baſe, ſmooth, of a ſhining green, and ſharply ſawed on their edges. The flowers terminate the ſtalks on a pretty long divided footſtalk, in a kind of little umbel, which is nodding at firſt but becomes erect, ſupporting five or ſix round, pentagonal, depreſſed capſules, filled with ſmall ſeeds.

A decoction or infuſion of this, has been uſed with conſiderable ſucceſs as a ſubſtitute for the Peruvian bark. The roots are ſaid to give eaſe in the tooth ach. This kind is called by the Indians *Phipſeſawa.*

PYRUS.

The PEAR-TREE.

Claſs 12. Order 4. Icoſandria Pentagynia.

THE *Empalement* is of one leaf, concave, half five-cleft, and permanent; the ſegments ſpreading.

The *Corolla* has five roundiſh, concave, large petals, inſerted in the empalement.

The *Filaments* are twenty, awl-ſhaped, ſhorter than the corolla, and inſerted in the empalement. The *Antheræ* ſimple.

The *Germen* is beneath. The *Styles* five, thread-form, the length of the ſtamina. The *Stigmas* ſimple.

The *Seed-veſſel* a *pome*, roundiſh, umbilicated and fleſhy, with five membranaceous cells.

The *Seeds* a few, oblong, obtuſe, ſharpened at the baſe, convex on one ſide and plane on the other.

To this Genus *belongs*

MALUS.

MALUS.

The APPLE-TREE.

Of which we have one Species, viz.

PYRUS-MALUS coronaria. *Virginian ſweet-ſcented Crab-Tree.*

This often grows to the height of twelve or fifteen feet, dividing into many ſtiff branches, ſet pretty thick with ſhort ſtiff ſpurs. The leaves are ſomewhat like thoſe of the Apple-tree, but often toothed, or largely and irregularly ſawed on their edges. The flowers generally come out thick upon the branches, upon pretty long dividing footſtalks; they are pretty large, of a beautiful bluſh colour, and fragrant odour at their firſt appearance. The fruit is ſmall, hard, roundiſh, umbilicated, and extremely acid. It is frequently uſed for conſerves, &c. There is ſaid to be a variety of this in Carolina with evergeen leaves, though I have never ſeen it.

QUERCUS.

The OAK-TREE.

Claſs 21, Order 8. Monoecia Polyandria.

*THE *Male* Flowers are diſpoſed in a looſe katkin.

The *Empalement* is of one leaf, four or five-parted; the diviſions are acute and often bifid.

They have no *Corolla.*

The *Filaments* are ſeveral, very ſhort. The *Antheræ* large and double.

*The *Female* are in cloſe buds, on the ſame plant with the Male.

The *Perianthium* is of one leaf, coriaceous, hemiſpherical, rough, and entire, ſcarce manifeſt in the flower.

There

There is no *Corolla*.

The *Germen* is egg-ſhaped and ſmall. The *Style* ſimple, five-cleft and longer than the empalement. The *Stigmas* are ſimple and permanent.

There is no *Seed-veſſel*, but an oval, columnar, ſmooth nut, ſhaved at the baſe and affixed in the ſhort calyx.

The Species *and* Varieties *with us, are many, which, I think, may be divided in the following manner, into*

* Quercus alba. *White Oak.*

1. QUERCUS alba. *Common American White Oak.*

This grows very common, and with age arrives to the ſize of a large tree of ſeventy or eighty feet in height, and of three, four, five, or more feet in diameter; dividing into many large branches, and covered with a whitiſh ſcaly bark. The leaves are narrowed towards the baſe, but ſpreading and deeply ſinuated obliquely, towards the ends; the ſinuſes obtuſe, the angles, or productions unequal in length, entire and obtuſe. They are of a glaucous, or light green underneath and have very ſhort footſtalks. The acorns are middling ſized, ſitting in ſmall ſhallow cups. There are ſome varieties of this, differing in the hardneſs and toughneſs of the timber, and ſomewhat in their acorns or fruit. It affords a hard, tough, uſeful and valuable timber, which is hewed into beams, &c. for frame buildings; ſawed into plank, &c. for ſhip building; and applied to various other uſeful purpoſes. Our ſwine are often wholly fatted upon the ſeveral kinds of acorns, but for theſe and Cheſnut Oak they ſeek moſt diligently.

2. QUERCUS

2. QUERCUS alba minor. *Barren White Oak.*

This grows generally upon poor, barren, or waſte land, riſing perhaps to the height of thirty or forty feet, covered with ſcaly greyiſh bark. The leaves are ſomewhat rough, but of a ſhining green above, ſomewhat paler underneath; they are ſinuated deeply, moſt obtuſely, and irregularly; the lobes or productions (if I may be allowed the expreſſion) are obtuſe, often ſomewhat angular, and very irregular. The acorns are ſmall and ſtriped. The timber is accounted very durable for poſts, to ſet in the earth; otherwiſe not much eſteemed unleſs for fuel.

3. QUERCUS alba paluſtris. *Swamp White Oak.*

This becomes a pretty large ſpreading tree, of two or three feet in diameter and of proportionable height. The bark is often rougher or more furrowed than the other kinds, and greyiſh coloured. The leaves are ſomewhat wedge-ſhaped or narrowed towards the baſe, and toothed on their edges and extremities. The acorns are larger and rounder than thoſe of the common White Oak, and have larger and thicker cups, ſupported often by pairs upon a long, ſtrong footſtalk.

** Quercus nigra. *Black Oak.*

4. QUERCUS nigra. *Common Pennſylvanian Black Oak.*

This grows to the height of ſixty or ſeventy feet, and to three or four feet in diameter, with large ſpreading branches. The leaves are large, ſpreading, and ſomewhat woolly; their footſtalks longer than thoſe of the White Oak. They are irregularly ly and ſometimes pretty deeply ſinuated, the angles or productions unequal, generally obtuſe, yet with their veins extending in a briſtly point. The acorns are roundiſh and not large, ſitting in thick ſcaly cups. There is, I think, a variety of this of much ſmaller growth, with larger leaves and differing ſomewhat in the fruit. Our common Black Oak is uſed much (where Cedar is ſcarce) for making ſhingles, and alſo for rails, &c.

5. QUERCUS nigra digitata. *Finger-leaved Black Oak.*

This grows naturally in low lands, riſing to the height of thirty or forty feet, with a trunk of conſiderable thickneſs, covered with a rough blackiſh bark. The leaves are ſinuated, or divided towards their extremities into two or three pretty long, ſomewhat finger-ſhaped lobes, of unequal length, with others ſhorter, ſometimes at the ſides; all of which end in a briſtly point. The acorns are ſmall, but the cups pretty large.

6. QUERCUS nigra trifida. *Maryland Black Oak.*

This grows naturally in Maryland, and other low lands, with a trunk of eighteen inches or two feet in diameter, and thirty or forty feet in height. The leaves are wedge-ſhaped, or narrowed towards the baſe, and three-pointed, with briſtly terminations. The acorns and cups reſemble the laſt mentioned.

7. QUERCUS nigra integrifolia. *Entire-leaved Black Oak.*

This grows about the ſize of the other low-land Black Oak, and is of the ſame appearance, except the leaves being ſomewhat inverſe egg-ſhaped, and often a little notched or indented on each ſide towards the extremity.

8. Quercus nigra pumila. *Dwarf Black Oak.*

This grows naturally upon poor barren ridges, riſing to the height of five or ſix feet, with a crooked, branching ſtem. The leaves are about three pointed, much reſembling thoſe of the Maryland Black Oak. The acorns are ſmall, and ſtand in ſmall ſhallow cups. This, I believe, is of little uſe or beauty.

*** Quercus rubra. *Red Oak.*

9. Quercus rubra maxima. *Largeſt Red Oak.*

This often becomes a large tree, of the height of ſeventy or eighty feet and of four, five, or ſometimes ſix feet in diameter; retaining its thickneſs to a conſiderable height, and without lateral branches, but ſpreading at the top. The leaves are large, obtuſely and but lightly ſinuated, the angles acute, each often terminating with ſeveral acute, briſtly points. The acorns are large and ſomewhat conical, ſitting in broad ſhallow cups. The timber is uſed for ſtaves, ſhingles, rails, &c.

10. Quercus rubra ramoſiſſima. *Water Red Oak.*

This grows moſt naturally by creek ſides, or in low wet places, riſing to the height of a pretty large tree; generally thick ſet with ſlender lateral branches, and covered with ſomewhat ſmooth, greyiſh coloured bark. The leaves are ſmall, obtuſely and deeply ly ſinuated, pretty uniformly, almoſt to the midrib; the angles or lobes are narrow, acute, and unequal, each terminating with ſeveral briſtly points. The acorns and cups are ſmall. This is generally known by the name of Water or Low Land Spaniſh Oak. The buts of theſe trees are often uſed for rimming of carriage wheels, &c.

11. QUERCUS rubra montana. *Upland Red Oak.*

This grows naturally upon higher and poorer land than the others, often attaining to fifty or ſixty feet in height. The bark is ſomewhat rough and lightiſh coloured. The leaves are deeply and obtuſely ſinuated, ſomewhat regularly; the angles ſomewhat bitrifid, or ending in ſeveral acute, briſtly points; their footſtalks are pretty long. The acorns and cups are middling ſized. The timber is generally worm eaten, or rotten at heart, therefore of little eſteem. It is likewiſe commonly known by the name of Spaniſh Oak; and, I think, has ſome varieties differing in the ſize of their fruit and leaves.

12. QUERCUS rubra nana. *Dwarf Barren Oak.*

This grows naturally upon dry barren ridges, and is found from five to ten feet high, generally growing very crooked. The leaves are ſmaller, but ſomewhat reſemble thoſe laſt deſcribed. The acorns and cups are ſmall, the acorns red at the baſe and ſtriped when taken firſt from their cups. It is called barren from its place of growth, but is generally almoſt covered with fruit, ſitting very cloſe on all ſides of the branches.

**** Quercus Phellos. *Willow-leaved Oak.*

13. QUERCUS Phellos anguſtifolia. *Narrow Willow-leaved Oak.*

This grows naturally in low lands, and to the height of fifty or ſixty feet, with a trunk of conſiderable ſize. The leaves are entire, ſmooth, oblong, and lance-ſhaped, of about three inches in length and half an inch in breadth, and have very ſhort footſtalks. The acorns and cups are ſmall. The timber is ſound and good.

14. QUERCUS Phellos latifolia. *Broad Willow-leaved Oak.*

This tree very much reſembles the other in every reſpect, except in having leaves of about double the width; and broader but perhaps ſhorter cups and acorns.

15. QUERCUS Phellos ſempervirens. *Evergreen Willow-leaved Oak.*

This grows naturally in Carolina, becoming a pretty large tree, of the height of forty feet or more. The leaves are perennial, entire, ſomewhat oval, ſpear-ſhaped, of a dark green colour and thick conſiſtence. The acorns are ſmall, oblong, ſitting in ſhort cups, and containing a very ſweet kernel. The timber is hard, tough and coarſe grained.

***** Quercus Prinus. *Chesnut-leaved Oak.*

16. Quercus Prinus. *Chesnut-leaved Oak.*

This grows naturally upon a light gravelly soil, frequently to forty feet or more in height, and above two feet in diameter; covered with a furrowed, lightish coloured bark. The leaves are somewhat oval and uniformly crenated on their edges, or rather sometimes obtusely toothed. The acorns are smooth and large, greenish coloured and sitting in shallow spreading cups. The timber somewhat approaches towards that of Chesnut in appearance, but affords very good fuel, rails, &c.

17. Quercus Prinus humilis. *Dwarf Chesnut or Chinquepin Oak.*

This generally rises with several shrubby, spreading stalks, to the height of two or three feet. The leaves are somewhat wedge-shaped and toothed, or slightly and obliquely sinuated. The acorns and cups pretty much resemble those of the large kind, but are considerably smaller.

It may not be improper here to make some remarks with respect to cutting, or felling of timber. Long experience, I think, hath sufficiently ascertained, that timber cut down in the spring of the year, when full of sap, and the leaves fully expanded; and also in the third or last quarter of the moon's age; is much more durable than when cut at any other time. Timber when full of sap and vigour, in all probability, contains also more oily particles, which, in proportion as they abound, are known to add to its durability. With regard to the influence of the moon, it may probably be accounted a superstitious ftitious or whimfical fancy, but that it materially affects timber is a fact well known to thofe who ftrip, or peel bark for the ufe of tanners; and when accounted for in one cafe, may probably throw fome light upon the other. But further, it is alfo a fact well known, that timber, whofe bark has been fufficiently feparated and peeled round at the but, in order for deading, as it is termed; if done in the decreafe of the moon, retains its greennefs often a confiderable time; but if in the increafe, withers in a much fhorter time. From hence, I think, we may conclude, that the fap or juice of trees, has a kind of monthly circulation, or revolution; afcending in the moon's decreafe, but defcending in the increafe. However, be this as it may, the falling of timber in the different phafis of the moon, is confidently afferted, from experience, to materially affect its durability.

RHODODENDRUM.

DWARF ROSE-BAY.

Clafs 10. Order 1. Decandria Monogynia.

THE *Empalement* is of one leaf, five parted and permanent.
The *Corolla* of one leaf, wheel-funnelled: the border fpreading: the divifions rounded.
The *Filaments* ten, thread-form, almoft the length of the corolla, and declined. The *Antheræ* oval.
The *Germen* five cornered, retufe. The *Style* thread-form, the length of the corolla. The *Stigma* obtufe.
The *Seed-veffel* ovate, angled, five cell'd.
The *Seeds* numerous and fmall.

We have, with us, but one Species, viz.

RHODO-

RHODODENDRUM maximum. *Pennsylvanian Mountain Laurel.*

This grows to the height of about six or eight feet, often with several stems from the same root. The leaves are oblong and entire, generally about four or five inches in length and one and a half or near two in breadth: of a thick consistence, and shining dark green on the upper side but lighter underneath, continuing their verdure all the year. The flowers are pretty large and of a pale rose colour, studded with spots of a deeper red, having their tubes a little bent. They are produced at the extremity of the former year's shoots, in roundish clusters, making a beautiful appearance. This is much and deservedly esteemed as a very beautiful, evergreen, flowering shrub.

R H U S.

S U M A C H.

Class 5. Order 3. Pentandria Trigynia.

THE *Empalement* is five-parted, beneath, erect, and permanent.

The *Corolla* of five petals, ovate and a little spreading.

The *Filaments* are five, very short. The *Antheræ* small, shorter than the corolla.

The *Germen* above, roundish, and the size of the corolla. The *Styles* scarce any. The *Stigmas* three, hearted, small.

The *Seed-vessel* a berry, roundish, and of one cell.

The *Seed* one, roundish, bony.

Obs. The Toxicodendron has smooth, striated berries: the kernel compressed and furrowed.

The Vernix is male and female upon different plants.

The Glabrum (and perhaps some others) is female and hermaphrodite on different plants.

The

The Species *with us, are,*

1. RHUS Copallinum. *Lentiſcus-leaved Sumach.*

This grows to the height of ſix, eight, or ſometimes ten feet, dividing into ſlender branches, and covered with ſpeckled bark. The leaves are winged, and compoſed of four or five pair of narrow, entire lobes, terminated by an odd one; joined to a common footſtalk; with decurrent, leaffy expanſions between each pair of lobes. The flowers are produced in looſe, compound panicles, of an herbaceous colour, and are ſucceeded by reddiſh ſeeds, ſprinkled with a greyiſh pounce. This grows naturally in a ſlaty, gravelly ſoil. The berries are very acid. There are ſome varieties of this, much reſembling it but of ſmaller growth, and with redder berries.

2. RHUS glabrum. *Smooth Pennſylvanian Sumach.*

This grows naturally in ſeveral of the northern States, riſing to the height of ſix or eight feet, dividing in a few thick, pithy and ſomewhat angled branches; covered with a ſmooth bark. The leaves are large and winged, compoſed of eight, nine, or ten pair of lobes, and an odd one; oblong, pointed and ſawed on their edges; of a pretty deep green on their upper ſides, but much lighter underneath and changing reddiſh in autumn. The flowers are hermaphrodite and female on ſeparate plants, and are produced in large, erect, compounded panicles, or thyrſi, terminating the branches; of an herbaceous colour; the hermaphrodite of which are largeſt and barren, but the female are ſucceeded by ſeeds with a red meally covering, of an acid taſte.

RHUS glabrum carolinenſe. *Carolinian Scarlet-flowering Sumach.*

This is a variety of the laſt deſcribed, but differing in having ſcarlet flowers.

RHUS glabrum canadenſe. *Canadian Red-flowering Sumach.*

This is alſo a variety of the ſame, growing naturally in Canada, with red flowers.

3. RHUS typhinum. *Stag's-horn Sumach.*

This grows naturally in Virginia and Pennſylvania, often riſing to the height of twelve or fifteen feet, with a trunk of ſix or eight inches in diameter; dividing at the top into ſeveral branches; which, when young, are covered with a ſoft, velvet-like down, reſembling that of a young ſtag's horn, both in colour and texture. The leaves are compoſed of ſix or ſeven pair of oblong lobes, terminated by an odd one, ending in acute points, and together with the midrib, a little hairy underneath. The flowers are produced in a cloſe, erect panicle or thyrſus; terminating the branches; they are of an herbaceous colour and are ſucceeded by ſeeds encloſed in a purple, woolly, ſucculent covering; making a fine appearance in the autumn.

4. RHUS canadenſe. *Canadian trifoliate Sumach.*

This grows naturally in Canada, and perhaps the northern parts of Pennſylvania. The ſtems are ſlender, riſing to the height of ſix or eight feet, and covered with a brown bark. The leaves are composed of three lobes, somewhat egg-shaped and joined to a common footstalk. The flowers are male and female on different plants.

To this Genus *is also added,*

TOXICODENDRON.

The POISON-TREE.

Of which we have,

1. Rhus-Toxicodendron Vernix. *Varnish-Tree, or Poison Ash.*

This rises with a pretty strong, erect stem, to the height of twelve or fourteen feet; dividing towards the top into several branches. The leaves are winged, and composed of three or four pair of lobes, terminated by an odd one; which are for the most part oval, spear-shaped, smooth, and of a lucid green on their upper side, but paler and a little hairy underneath; their footstalks changing of a purple colour in autumn. The male and female flowers are produced upon different trees, and are disposed in loose panicles, coming out from the bosom of the leaves; of an herbaceous colour. The female are succeeded by small, roundish seeds, of a lightish colour when ripe. This is allowed to be the same with the true Varnish-tree of Japan; where it is collected in great quantities, by making incisions in the trees and placing vessels underneath to receive the milky juice, which hardens and becomes the true varnish; much used in various kinds of curious workmanship. This, in all probability, might be collected here equal in quality with that of Japan and to considerable advantage. This tree ought to be be handled with caution, as it is very poiſonous to many people.

2. RHUS-TOXICODENDRON toxicodendrum. *Poiſon-Oak.*

This has a low, ſhrubby ſtalk, ſeldom riſing above three or four feet. The leaves are trifoliate, with pretty long footſtalks, the lobes are entire, ſmooth and ſomewhat heart-ſhaped. The flowers come out from the ſides of the ſtalks, in looſe panicles of an herbaceous colour; ſmall, and not always hermaphrodite. They are ſucceeded by roundiſh, channelled, ſmooth berries, of a yellowiſh grey colour when ripe.

3. RHUS-TOXICODENDRON radicans. *Poiſon-Vine.*

This riſes with many ſhrubby climing ſtems, attaching themſelves to every neighbouring ſupport; and often riſing to the height of twenty or thirty feet, with a ſtem of two or three inches in diameter; ſending off many branches. The leaves are trifoliate, and have pretty long footſtalks: the lobes are ſomewhat oval and pointed, often ſomewhat toothed. The flowers are produced in ſhort panicles from the ſides of the branches, and are ſucceeded by roundiſh berries, of a browniſh colour when ripe.

RIBES.

The CURRANT-BUSH.

Claſs 5. Order 1. Pentandria Monogynia.

THE *Empalement* is of one leaf, part five-cleft and bellied: the diviſions oblong, concave, coloured, reflexed and permanent. The

The *Corolla* is of five petals, ſmall, obtuſe and erect, adjoined to the margin of the empalement.

The *Filaments* are five, awl-ſhaped, erect and inſerted in the calyx. The *Antheræ* are incumbent, compreſſed, and gaping at the margin.

The *Germen* roundiſh and beneath. The *Style* bifid. The *Stigmas* obtuſe.

The *Seed veſſel* a berry, globous, umbilicated and of one cell, with two receptacles, lateral, oppoſite and longitudinal.

The *Seeds* many, roundiſh, and ſomewhat compreſſed.

The Species, *with us, are,*

* Ribeſia inermia. *Currant-Trees.*

1. RIBES nigrum pennſylvanicum. *Pennſylvanian Black Currants.*

This grows to the height of the common cultivated Currant, but the ſtalks are generally more ſlender and covered with a darkiſh, ſmooth bark. The leaves have the ſame reſemblance but are ſmaller. The flowers grow in looſe bunches, and are ſucceeded by oblong, black fruit when ripe.

** Groſſulariæ aculeatæ. *Gooſe-berries.*

2. RIBES oxycanthoides. *Mountain Wild Gooſeberry.*

Theſe grow to the ſize of the common Gooſe-berry, but have ſmaller ſtems and not branching ſo much; but near the earth are often prickly on all ſides. The leaves are ſmaller but have the ſame appearance. The fruit is alſo much ſmaller but of an agreeable taſte when ripe. This either by a little culture becomes ſmooth, otherwiſe we have a different kind, not more prickly than the common.

3. RIBES

3. RIBES cynosbati. *Prickly fruited Wild Goose-berry.*

This grows naturally in Canada and the upper parts of Pennsylvania; and much resembles the other, except in having its fruit covered on all sides with softish prickles.

ROBINIA.

ROBINIA, or FALSE-ACACIA.

Class 17. Order 3. Diadelphia Decandria.

THE *Empalement* is of one leaf, small, bell-shaped, and four-toothed: the three inferior slender; the superior fourth of double the width, and slightly emarginated; all equal in length.

The *Corolla* Butterfly-shaped.

The *Standard* roundish, large, spreading and obtuse.

The *Wings* oblong, ovate, free: with very short, obtuse appendages.

The *Keel* almost semi-orbiculate, compressed, obtuse, and the length of the wings.

The *Stamina* are *Filaments* in two sets, or bodies; (one simple, the other nine-cleft) rising above. The *Antheræ* roundish.

The *Germen* cylindrical, oblong. The *Style* thread-form, bent upward. The *Stigma* villous before, at the apex of the style.

The *Seed-vessel* large, compressed, gibbous, and long.

The *Seeds* few, kidney-form.

The Species *with us, are,*

1. ROBINIA Pseud-Acacia. *White flowering Robinia, or Locust-Tree.*

This grows naturally in several of these States; rising to the height of forty or fifty feet, with a trunk of eighteen or twenty inches in diameter, dividing

viding into many branches which are armed with ſhort, ſtrong ſpines. The bark is darkiſh coloured and rough. The leaves are winged and generally compoſed of eight or ten pair of ſmall, oval lobes, terminated by an odd one; entire, of a bright green and ſitting cloſe to the midrib. The flowers are produced from the ſides of the branches in long pendulous bunches, each having a ſeparate footſtalk; they are white, of a butterfly ſhape and ſweet ſmelling; and are ſucceeded by compreſſed pods, of three or four inches in length and half an inch in width, containing ſeveral hard, kidney-ſhaped ſeeds. The timber is very durable, and uſed for poſts to ſet in the earth, and other purpoſes; therefore, the propagation of it might be well worthy of attention. Its natural place of growth is in a rich moiſt ſoil.

2. ROBINIA roſea. *Roſe coloured Robinia.*

This ſpreads much from its running roots, ſending up weak branching ſtalks, to the height of ſix or eight feet, but often flowering much ſmaller. The whole plant, with the footſtalks of the leaves and flowers, are cloſely armed with ſoft, purpliſh ſpines. The leaves are winged and compoſed of five or ſix pair of oval, concave lobes, terminated by an odd one, with their midribs protruding in ſhort briſtly points. The flowers are larger than thoſe of the other kind and of a Peach bloſſom colour, with their ſtamina diſtinctly in two bodies; whereas thoſe of the other are frequently all joined at the baſe. This is a beautiful flowering ſhrub, ſometimes flowering twice or more in a ſeaſon, but ſeldom producing ſeeds. There are ſeveral other varieties differing ſomewhat in their pods or colour of their flowers.

ROSA.

R O S A.

The R O S E - B U S H.

Claſs 12. Order 5. Icoſandria Polygynia.

THE *Empalement* is of one leaf. The *tube* bellied; narrowed at the neck; the *border* ſpreading, five parted and globous: the diviſions long, narrow and pointed.

The *Corolla* is compoſed of five petals, heart-ſhaped, the length of the empalement, and inſerted in its neck.

The *Stamina* are very many, capillary, very ſhort, and inſerted in the neck of the empalement. The *Stigmas* obtuſe.

The *Seed-veſſel* is fleſhy, top-ſhaped, coloured, and of one cell.

The *Seeds* numerous, oblong, hairy, and joined within on all ſides of the Seed-veſſel.

The Species, *native with us, are,*

1. ROSA carolinenſis. *Wild Virginian Roſe.*

This riſes with ſeveral ſtalks to the height of five or ſix feet, ſomewhat prickly, as are alſo the foot-ſtalks of the leaves and flowers. The leaves are compoſed of four or five pair of lobes terminated with an odd one, which are ſomewhat ſpear-ſhaped and ſawed on their edges. The flowers are ſingle, of a red colour and late coming.

2. ROSA paluſtris. *Swamp Pennſylvanian Roſe.*

This grows generally in ſwamps; riſing to the height of four or five feet, with erect, and very prickly ſtems, branching out at top in a regular head. The leaves are compoſed of three pair of lobes, terminated by an odd one, of an oblong, oval ſhape

ſhape and ſlightly ſerrated, joined to a common footſtalk with a few ſpines underneath. The flowers are ſingle and of a damaſk colour; the hips or ſeed-veſſels are of a dark red, roundiſh, depreſſed, prickly or briſtly, and very clammy to the touch.

3. ROSA humilis. *Dwarf Pennſylvanian Roſe.*

This riſes with ſeveral ſlender ſtems to the height of two or three feet; covered with a browniſh green bark, and armed with a few ſharp ſpines. The leaves are compoſed of three or four pair of lobes, and an odd one, of an oblong egg-ſhape and ſharply ſawed on their edges. The leaves of the flower cup have often linear, leaffy elongations. The flowers are ſingle and of a pale reddiſh colour.

4. ROSA pennſylvanica plena. *Double Pennſylvanian Roſe.*

This very much reſembles the laſt deſcribed in growth and appearance, except in having a double flower.

RUBUS.

The RASPBERRY BUSH and BRAMBLE.

Claſs 12. Order 5. Icoſandria Polygynia.

THE *Empalement* is of one leaf, five-parted: the diviſions oblong, ſpreading and permanent.

The *Corolla* is of five petals, roundiſh, ſomewhat ſpreading, of the length of the Empalement and inſerted into it.

The *Filaments* are numerous, ſhorter than the petals, and inſerted in the Empalement. The *Antheræ* are roundiſh and compreſſed.

The *Germen* are numerous. The *Styles* ſmall, capillary, and ariſing from the ſides of the germen. The *Stigmas* ſimple and permanent.

The

The *Seed-veſſel* a compound berry: the *acini* roundiſh, collected in a convex head, concave beneath; and each with one cell.
The *Seeds* ſolitary and oblong; their receptacle conical.

The Species, *with us, are,*

1. RUBUS fruticoſus. *Common Blackberry Buſh.*

This riſes generally (with ſeveral ſtalks from the ſame root) to the height of four or five feet, but ſometimes to eight or ten: which are ſomewhat angled, and pretty thick ſet with ſharp prickles. The leaves are compoſed of three lobes, the ſide ones of which are often divided; moſtly egg-ſhaped, pointed, acutely and unequally ſawed on their edges, a little hairy underneath, and joined to a pretty long prickly footſtalk, the middle one extending ſome little diſtance from the others. This is generally well furniſhed with flowers, which often ſtand upon panicled, or divided footſtalks, and are ſucceeded by black fruit when ripe.

2. RUBUS hiſpidus. *American Dewberry Buſh.*

This is much ſmaller than the other, having ſeveral ſlender weak ſtems, which often trail on the ground to a conſiderable diſtance. The leaves very much reſemble thoſe of the Blackberry, but are generally ſmaller. The fruit is alſo ſmaller, rounder and blacker; and ſupported upon long, ſimple, prickly footſtalks.

3. RUBUS canadenſis. *Smooth ſtalked Canadian Bramble.*

This is ſaid to grow in Canada with purpliſh ſtalks without prickles. The leaves are fingered; compoſed of ten, five, and three lobes, which are very ſlender, lance-ſhaped, and ſharply ſerrated.

4. RUBUS occidentalis. *American Raſpberry.*

This riſes with a round prickly ſtalk, of ſeven or eight feet in length, which often deſcends again to the earth in a ſemi-circular manner, ſometimes taking root. The ſtalks are covered with a thin bluiſh ſcum or miſt, and furniſhed with trifoliate leaves. The lobes are ſomewhat heart, or egg-ſhaped; cut and ſawed on their edges, whitiſh and downy underneath, the lateral ones ſometimes divided, the common footſtalk pretty long, and the middle or terminal lobe a little ſubtended. The flowers are produced at the extremity of the branches in a kind of racemus or bunch, and are ſucceeded by ſmall fruit of a reddiſh black colour when ripe; the *acini* of which are joined, parting entire from the conical receptacle.

5. RUBUS odoratus. *Virginian Roſe-flowering Raſpberry.*

This riſes with upright woody ſtalks, without prickles, to the height of three or four feet, covered with a brown ſcaly bark. The leaves are ſingle, large, palmated or divided into five or more pointed lobes, ſharply ſawed on their edges, a little hairy, and joined to pretty long, hairy footſtalks. The flowers are produced in a kind of panicle at the extremity of the branches, of a curdled reddiſh colour; reſembling

resembling a small single Rose, both in their petals, and divisions of their flower cups which are villous, and terminate in leaffy elongations. This grows naturally on rocky mountains in Pennsylvania and Virginia, and makes an agreeable appearance by a long succession of rose-shaped flowers.

SALIX.

The WILLOW-TREE.

Class 22. Order 2. Dioecia Diandria.

* THE *Male* Flowers are dispofed in a common, oblong, imbricated katkin; with an involucrum formed of the bud.
The *Scales* are one-flowered, oblong, plain, and spreading.
It hath no petals; but a very small, cylindrical, truncated, honey-bearing Gland, or Nectarium, in the center of the flower.
The *Filaments* are two, straight, and thread form. The *Antheræ* are twin, and four-cell'd.
* The *Female* have a katkin and scales as the male.
The *Petals* none.
The *Germen* ovate, and lessened into a *Style* scarce distinct, somewhat longer than the Scales of the flower-cup. The *Stigmas* two, bifid and erect.
The *Seed-vessel* a *capsule*, ovate-awl-shaped, of one cell and two valves: the valves revolute.
The *Seeds* are numerous, ovate, very small, and crowned with a simple hairy Pappus.

The Species, *native with us, are,*

* *With smooth serrated leaves.*

1. SALIX nigra. *Rough American Willow.*

This rises often with a leaning or crooked trunk to the height of about twenty feet, covered with a dark

dark coloured, rough bark. The leaves are ſmooth and of equal colour on both ſides; narrow, lance-ſhaped, and very ſlightly ſerrated. The katkins are long and ſlender.

** *With ſerrated villoſe leaves.*

2. Salix ſericea. *Ozier, or Silky leaved Willow.*

This riſes generally to the height of eight or ten feet, with many ſhrubby ſtalks, covered with pretty ſmooth, dark, greeniſh bark. The leaves are ſhorter and ſomewhat broader than the other kind, lance-ſhaped, ſilky underneath, and very ſlightly ſerrated on the edges.

*** *With entire villoſe leaves.*

3. Salix humilis. *Dwarf Willow.*

This ſeldom riſes above three or four feet, with greeniſh, ſomewhat downy ſtalks. The leaves are larger than the other kinds, entire, oblong, ſomewhat oval, and glaucous or whitiſh underneath. There are ſome varieties of larger growth, belonging either to this or the laſt mentioned kind.

SAMBUCUS.

The ELDER-TREE.

Claſs 5. Order 3. Pentandria Trigynia.

THE *Empalement* is of one leaf, above, very ſmall, five-parted, and permanent.

The *Corolla* is of one petal, concave wheel-ſhaped, part five-cleft, obtuſe, the diviſions reflexed.

The

The *Filaments* five, awl-ſhaped, the length of the corolla. The *Antheræ* roundiſh.

The *Germen* beneath, ovate, obtuſe. The *Style* none, but in its place a bellied *Gland*. The *Stigmas* three, obtuſe.

The *Seed-veſſel* a roundiſh berry of one cell.

The *Seeds* three, angular on one ſide and convex on the other.

The Species, *with us, are,*

1. SAMBUCUS nigra. *American Black-berried Elder.*

This riſes generally to the height of ſix or eight feet, with a ſtem ſometimes of two or three inches in diameter. The leaves are generally compoſed of three pair of lobes and an odd one, which are ſomewhat oval, pointed, ſharply ſawed on their edges, a little hairy on both ſides, light coloured underneath and joined to pretty large, channelled footſtalks, placed oppoſite. The flowers are produced at the extremities of the ſame year's ſhoots in a kind of umbel, of five principal parts, again divided: they are white and are ſucceeded by berries which are blackiſh when ripe. An infuſion of the inner bark is purgative. From the berries may be prepared a ſpirit, a wine, and an oil, which promote urine, perſpiration and ſweat.

2. SAMBUCUS canadenſis. *Canadian Red-berried Elder.*

This grows naturally upon Mountain ſides, or moiſt, rich, ſhaded places, in the back parts of Pennſylvania. It has much the appearance of the other kind, but produces red berries, which are ripe the latter end of June, at the time the other is in flower.

SMILAX.

SMILAX.

ROUGH BINDWEED, or GREEN BRIAR.

Claſs 22. Order 6. Dioecia Hexandria.

* THE *Male* have *Empalements* of ſix leaves, of a ſpreading bell-ſhape; the leaves are oblong, joined at the baſe, ſpreading and reflexed at the apex.
The *Corolla* none.
The *Filaments* are ſix, ſimple. The *Antheræ* oblong.
* The *Female* have *Empalements* as the male, deciduous.
The *Corolla* none.
The *Germen* ovate. The *Styles* three, very ſmall. The *Stigmas* oblong, reflexed, downy.
The *Seed-veſſel* a globoſe berry, of three cells.
The *Seeds* two, globoſe.

The Species, *with us, are,*

* *With a ſquare prickly ſtem.*

1. SMILAX Sarſaparilla. *Ivy leaved rough Bindweed, or Sarſaparilla.*

This grows naturally in Virginia and to the ſouthward, riſing up with prickly, angular ſtalks. The leaves are without prickles, oval ſhaped, pointed, and three nerved.

2. SMILAX virginiana. *Lanceolate-leaved rough Bindweed.*

The ſtalks of this are ſlender, angular and prickly. The leaves are without ſpines, ſpear-ſhaped and pointed; their baſes not eared.

** *With*

** *With a round prickly ſtem.*

3. SMILAX rotundifolia. *Canadian round leaved Smilax.*

The ſtalks of this are round and winding, with a few ſtraight ſpines. The leaves are heart-ſhaped, without ſpines, five-nerved, having ſhort footſtalks with two ſlender claſpers.

4. SMILAX laurifolia. *Bay leaved rough Bindweed.*

This hath a round ſtalk, armed with prickles or ſpines. The leaves are of an oval lance-ſhape, without ſpines, and of thicker conſiſtence than thoſe of the other ſpecies. The flowers are ſmall and whitiſh, the berries black when ripe.

5. SMILAX tamnoides. *Bryony leaved rough Bindweed.*

The ſtems of this are armed with prickles and round; climing upon the neighbouring trees for ſupport. The leaves are without ſpines, of an oblong heart-ſhape and five nerved. The berries are black.

6. SMILAX caduca. *Three-nerved-leaved rough Bindweed.*

This riſes with round, naked, winding ſtalks, armed with many ſtraight, black pointed ſpines and covered with a green bark. The leaves are ovate, pointed, three nerved and annual. The berries black.

*** *With a ſquare ſmooth ſtem.*

7. SMILAX bona nox. *Carolinian prickly leaved Smilax.*

The ſtalks of this are angular and without ſpines. The leaves are broad, and ciliated or ſet upon the margin with ſpines. There is alſo a variety with narrow rough leaves, eared at the baſe and angular.

**** *With a ſmooth round ſtem.*

8. SMILAX lanceolata. *Red berried Virginian Smilax.*

The ſtalks of this are ſmooth and round. The leaves are without ſpines and lance-ſhaped. The berries red coloured.

9. SMILAX Pſeudo China. *Baſtard China.*

This hath ſmooth round ſtalks. The leaves are without ſpines, thoſe on the ſtalks heart-ſhaped, but on the branches lance-ſhaped. The berries are black and ſupported on very long footſtalks.

SORBUS.

The SERVICE TREE, QUICKBEAM, or MOUNTAIN ASH.

Claſs 12. Order 3. Icoſandria Trigynia.

THE *Empalement* is of one leaf, concave-ſpreading, five-parted and permanent.

The *Corolla* is of five petals, roundiſh, concave and inſerted in the Empalement.

The *Filaments* twenty, awl-ſhaped, and inſerted in the Empalement. The *Antheræ* roundiſh.

The

The *Germen* beneath. The *Styles* three, thread-form, and erect. The *Stigmas* headed.
The *Seed-vessel* a berry, soft, globose, and umbilicated.
The *Seeds* three, somewhat oblong, distinct, and cartilaginous.

The Species, *with us, but one, viz.*

SORBUS americana. *American Service Tree.*

This grows naturally upon the mountains towards Canada; rising to the height of about fifteen or eighteen feet, with an erect stem dividing into several branches. The leaves are winged, composed of eight or nine pair of lobes, terminated by an odd one; which are narrow and sawed on their edges. The flowers are produced at the extremity of the branches in form of an umbel, and are succeeded by roundish berries of a red colour when ripe.

S P I R Æ A.

S P I R Æ A.

Class 12. Order 4. Icosandria Pentagynia.

THE *Empalement* is of one leaf, half five-cleft, and plane at the base: the divisions acute; permanent.
The *Corolla* of five petals, oblong-rounded, and inserted in the calyx.
The *Filaments* above twenty, thread-form, shorter than the corolla, and inserted in the calyx. The *Antheræ* roundish.
The *Germen* five or more. The *Styles* as many, thread-form, and the length of the Stamina. The *Stigmas* headed.
The *Seed-vessels* capsules, oblong, sharp-pointed, compressed and two valved.
The *Seeds* few, sharp-pointed and small.
Obs. S. opulifolia has three Styles.

The

The Species, *with us, are,*

1. Spiræa hypericifolia. *Canadian Spiræa, or Hypericum-frutex.*

This rifes generally to the height of four or five feet, dividing into many flender branches, and covered with a dark brown bark. The leaves are oblong, entire, and fmooth, refembling thofe of St. John's-wort, and placed oppofite. The flowers are yellow, and difpofed in fmall umbels, fitting clofe to the ftalks, each having a long, flender footftalk; and are fucceeded by oblong, pointed capfules, filled with fmall feeds. This makes a very good appearance when in flower.

2. Spiræa opulifolia. *Guelder Rofe-leaved Spiræa, or Nine-Bark.*

This rifes with many fhrubby branching ftalks, covered with a brown fcaly bark, to the height of five or fix feet. The leaves are fomewhat three parted, the two fide divifions or lobes fmall, obtufe and near the bafe; the middle one large and pointed; they are alfo flightly crenated and fawed on their edges. The flowers are produced at the extremity of the branches, in form of a corymbus or clufter: they are white with fome fpots of pale red, and are fucceeded by clufters of greenifh, inflated capfules.

Spiræa caroliniana. *Carolinian Guelder Rofe-leaved Spiræa.*

This is a variety of the former, and refembles it much in growth and appearance.

3. SPIRÆA tomentoſa. *Scarlet flowered Philadelphian Spiræa.*

This grows naturally in Pennſylvania; riſing with ſlender, branching ſtalks to the height of three or four feet, having a purple bark, covered with a grey meally down. The leaves are ſmall, ſpear-ſhaped, unequally ſawed on their edges, of a bright green on their upper ſides, but downy and veined underneath. The flowers terminate the branches in form of a racemus or bunch; they are ſmall and of a beautiful red colour.

4. SPIRÆA tomentoſa alba. *White flowered Philadelphian Spiræa.*

This is a variety of the former; riſing with ſlender ſtalks to the height of four or five feet. The leaves are ſmall and of thin texture, of an oblong oval, or ſomewhat wedge ſhape, ſlightly and ſharply ſawed on their edges, and a little downy on both ſides. The flowers are produced in manner of the former, of a beautiful white, making a pretty appearance. This is called Indian Pipe Shank, from the pithy ſtems being uſed by the natives for that purpoſe.

STAPHYLÆA.

BLADDER-NUT-TREE.

Claſs 5. Order 3. Pentandria Trigynia.

THE *Empalement* is five-parted, concave, roundiſh, coloured, and almoſt the ſize of the corolla.

The *Corolla* is five petal'd, oblong, erect, and like the calyx.

The *Nectarium* concave and pitcher-ſhape in the bottom of the flower.

The

The *Stamina* are five, oblong, erect, and the length of the calyx. The *Antheræ* simple.

The *Germen* thickish, three-parted. The *Styles* three, simple and a little longer than the stamina. The *Stigmas* obtuse and contiguous.

The *Seed-vessel* three *Capsules*, inflated, flaccid, joined by longitudinal sutures; and with pointed tops gaping inwardly.

The *Seeds* are few, hard, and roundish, joined to the interior sutures.

The Species, *with us*, *but one*, viz.

STAPHYLÆA trifoliata. *Three-leaved Bladder-nut-Tree.*

This rises generally to the height of eight or ten feet, dividing into many branches, placed opposite. The bark of the stem and old branches are of a greyish colour, but of the young shoots of a light green. The leaves are trifoliate, the middle lobe having a footstalk; the lobes are oval, lance-shaped, slightly and sharply sawed on their edges, and joined to pretty long common footstalks, placed opposite. The flowers are produced upon pretty long, panicled footstalks; they are white and are succeeded by pretty large, three-sided bladders or capsules, enclosing a few roundish, hard seeds.

STEWARTIA.

STEWARTIA.

Class 16. Order 5. Monadelphia Polyandria.

THE *Empalement* is of one leaf, five parted and spreading; the divisions ovate, concave, and permanent.

The *Corolla* consists of five petals, inverse-ovate, spreading, equal and large.

The

The *Filaments* are numerous, filiform, ſhorter than the corolla, joined in a cylinder below, and to the petals at the baſe. The *Antheræ* are roundiſh and incumbent.

The *Germen* roundiſh and hairy. The *Style* filiform, the length of the Stamina. The *Stigma* five cleft.

The *Seed-veſſel* a juiceleſs *pome*, five lobed, and five cell'd.

The *Seeds* are ſolitary, ovate and compreſſed.

The Species *but one*, viz.

STEWARTIA Malacodendron. *Virginian Stewartia.*

This grows naturally in Virginia; riſing with ſtrong ſtems to the height of ten or twelve feet, and covered with a brown bark. The leaves are oval and ſomewhat ſpear-ſhaped, moſt ſlightly ſerrated and villoſe underneath. The flowers are large and white, produced ſingly, and ſitting cloſe upon the ſmall branches. The ſeed-veſſels are dry, ſomewhat conical, ligneous capſules, having five ſharp angles, and five cells, each containing one oblong ſmooth ſeed. This makes a beautiful appearance when well filled with its large white flowers.

S T Y R A X.

The S T O R A X - T R E E.

Claſs 11. Order 1. Dodecandria Monogynia.

THE *Empalement* is of one leaf, cylindrical, erect, ſhort and five-toothed.

The *Corolla* is of one petal, funnel-form. The *tube* is ſhort, cylindrical, and the length of the calyx. The *border* five-parted, large and ſpreading: the diviſions lance-ſhaped and obtuſe.

The *Filaments* are erect, placed in a circle, more than twelve, ſcarce joined at the baſe, awl-ſhaped and inſerted in the corolla. The *Antheræ* are oblong and ſtraight.

The

The *Germen* beneath. The *Style* ſimple, the length of the ſtamina. The *Stigma* lopped.
The *Seed-veſſel* a *drupe*, roundiſh and of one cell.
The *Seeds* two nuts, roundiſh, pointed, convex on one ſide and plane on the other.

The Species, *with us*, *but one*, viz.

STYRAX americana. *Carolinian Storax-Tree.*

This grows naturally in Carolina; riſing with a pretty ſtrong ſtem to the height of ten or twelve feet, covered with a ſmooth browniſh bark, and dividing into many ſlender branches. The leaves are pretty large, oval ſhaped, a little pointed, ſcarce obſervably toothed, of a deep green, and a little downy on the upper ſurface, but lighter and much more downy underneath; having ſhort footſtalks, which together with the young ſhoots, are alſo woolly or downy. The flowers are produced upon the ſmall branches, in a kind of racemus or bunch; ſupporting a few ſcattered flowers, which are white, pendulous, and have each ten ſtamina and ſomewhat the fragrance of an Orange flower. They are ſucceeded by roundiſh ſeed-veſſels, each containing two roundiſh, pointed nuts or ſeeds.

T A X U S.

The Y E W - T R E E.

Claſs 22. Order 12. Dioecia Monadelphia.

* THE *Male* Flowers have no *Empalements*, but a bud of four leaves ſomewhat like one.
They have no *Corolla*.
The *Filaments* are numerous, joined beneath in a column, and longer than the bud. The *Antheræ* are depreſſed, obtuſe at the margin, eight-cleft, gaping on every ſide at the baſe

(and

(and having caſt their farina) plane, targetted, and remarkable for their eight-cleft margin.

* The *Female Empalements* are as in the Male.

They have no *Corolla.*

The *Germen* is ovate and pointed. The *Style* none. The *Stigma* obtuſe.

The *Seed-veſſel* is formed of the lengthened receptacle, into a globoſe, ſucculent, coloured covering or berry, open at top.

The *Seed* one, oblong-ovate, the apex protruding out of the berry.

We have, native but one Species, viz.

TAXUS canadenſis. *Canadian Yew-Tree.*

This ſhrub is of low growth, but divided into many branches ſpreading on every ſide. The leaves are narrow, ſtiff, linear, pointed, and evergreen; thick ſet upon all ſides of the branches, but inclining upwards. The flowers come out thick upon the ſides of the branches and are ſucceeded by oval, red, ſucculent berries, open at top; and encloſing an oval brown ſeed. This is a beautiful evergreen ſhrub, capable of being formed into any ſhape.

THUYA.

ARBOR VITÆ, or TREE OF LIFE.

Claſs 21. Order 9. Monoecia Monodelphia.

* THE *Male* Flowers are diſpoſed in oval katkins, and are placed upon a common footſtalk in triple oppoſition; each one having for its baſe

A *Scale* ſomewhat ovate, concave and obtuſe.

No *Corolla*, but

Four *Filaments* in each flower, ſcarce manifeſt, and as many *Antheræ*, adjoined to the baſe of the ſcaly cup.

* The *Female* flowers are upon the ſame plant, in ſomewhat ovate Cones, compoſed of oppoſite Scales, which are two flowered, ovate and convex.

No *Corolla*.

The *Germen* is very ſmall. The *Style* awl-ſhaped. The *Stigma* ſimple.

The *Seed-veſſel* a Cone, oblong-ovate, obtuſe, and gaping longitudinally: the *Scales* are oblong, nearly equal, convex outwardly and obtuſe.

The *Seeds* are oblong, begirt longitudinally with a membranaceous, end-bitten wing.

The Species, *with us, but one,* viz.

THUYA occidentalis. *American Arbor Vitæ.*

This grows naturally in Canada, and other northern parts of America; riſing to the height of thirty or forty feet, with a pretty ſtrong ſtem, ſending off many branches, which are produced irregularly and ſtand almoſt horizontally. The bark of young trees is of a dark brown and ſmooth, but afterward becomes cracked and leſs ſmooth. The young branches are flat, and covered with very ſmall leaves, lying over each other like ſcales of fiſh. The cones are ſmall and looſe, containing but few oblong, winged ſeeds.

THUYA variegata. *Striped leaved Arbor Vitæ.*

This is a variety of the firſt, differing in having ſtriped or variegated leaves.

THUYA odorata. *American Sweet-ſcented Arbor Vitæ.*

This is alſo a variety of the ſame, agreeing with it in growth and appearance; but differing in its leaves or ſmall branches, being of an agreeable, or ſweet ſcent, when bruiſed.

T I L I A.

The LIME, or LINDEN-TREE.

Claſs 13. Order 6. Polyandria Hexagynia.

THE *Empalement* is five parted, concave, coloured, almoſt the length of the corolla, and deciduous.

The *Corolla* is of five petals, oblong, obtuſe and notched at the end.

The *Filaments* are many, (thirty and upwards) awl-ſhaped, and the length of the corolla. The *Antheræ* are ſimple.

The *Germen* roundiſh. The *Style* filiform, the length of the ſtamina. The *Stigma* obtuſely five-ſided.

The *Seed-veſſel* a *Capſule*, coriaceous, globoſe, five-cell'd, five-valved, and gaping at the baſe.

The *Seed* ſolitary and roundiſh.

Obſ. The Capſule appears to have but one cell and one ſeed, the other four being abortive.

The American Tilia has five Scales placed round the bud and joined to the claws of the corolla.

The Species *with us, are,*

1. TILIA americana. *American black Lime, or Linden-Tree.*

This often becomes a tree of a large ſize, covered with a dark brown bark, and dividing into many branches. The leaves are large, heart-ſhaped, pointed, and ſawed on their edges, of a deep green on their upper ſides, but paler and a little hairy underneath; and ſtanding on long footſtalks. The flowers are produced upon the ſmall branches, and are remarkable for having an oblong *bractea* or floral leaf upon each footſtalk; they are of an herbaceous colour, having narrow petals furniſhed with nectaries at the baſe. The capſules are round, a little hairy

hairy and about the ſize of a ſmall pea, having each one roundiſh ſeed.

2. TILIA caroliniana. *Carolinian oblique-leaved Lime-Tree.*

This is of ſmaller growth than the former, riſing commonly to the height of about forty feet, with a trunk of eighteen inches or more in diameter: covered with a lightiſh and ſomewhat furrowed bark, and ſending off many branches. The leaves are ſmaller and ſmoother than thoſe of the other kind, ſomewhat heart-ſhaped, ending in long points, unequal at the baſe, or larger on one ſide of the midrib than the other, and ſlightly ſawed on their edges. The bunches of flowers ſtand upon long ſlender footſtalks, furniſhed with floral leaves. The flowers are ſmall, and have narrow, pointed petals, furniſhed with nectaries or ſcales at the baſe; they diffuſe a fragrant odour, and are continually haunted by bees during their continuance. An infuſion of the flowers of Lime-tree has been uſed with ſucceſs in an Epilepſy. The timber is too ſoft for any ſtrong purpoſes, therefore, chiefly uſed by turners, carvers, &c. alſo, by architects in framing models of buildings, &c.

TILLANDSIA.

TILLANDSIA.

Claſs 6. Order 1. Hexandria Monogynia.

THE *Empalement* is of one leaf, three-parted, oblong and permament: the diviſions oblong-lanced, and ſharp-pointed.

The *Corolla* tubulous and of one petal. The *tube* long and bellied. The *border* three-cleft, obtuſe, erect and ſmall.

The

The *Filaments* are fix, as long as the tube of the corolla. The *Antheræ* acute, and incumbent in the neck of the corolla.
The *Germen* is oblong, and pointed on every fide. The *Style* filiform, and the length of the ftamina. The *Stigma* three-cleft and obtufe.
The *Seed-veffel* a *Capfule*, which is long, obtufely three-fided, pointed with about one cell and three valves.
The *Seeds* are many, joined to a very long, capillary pappus or down.

The Species, *with us, but one,* viz.

TILLANDSIA ufneoides. *Carolinian Tillandfia.*

This is a parafite plant; or growing upon the branches of trees and hanging down with very flender, rough, branching threads or ftalks, in manner of mofs. The leaves are whitifh and hoary.

ULMUS.

The ELM-TREE.

Clafs 5. Order 2. Pentrandria Digynia.

THE *Empalement* is of one leaf, top-fhaped, and wrinkled. The *border* five parted, erect, coloured within, and permanent.
The *Corolla* none.
The *Filaments* five, awl-fhaped, and twice the length of the calyx. The *Antheræ* four-furrowed, erect and fhort.
The *Germen* orbicular and erect. The *Styles* two, fhorter than the ftamina and reflexed. The *Stigmas* downy.
The *Seed-veffel* a *drupe*, oval compreffed, membranaceous and juicelefs.
The *Seed* one, roundifh and lightly compreffed.

The Species, *with us, are,*

1. ULMUS

1. Ulmus americana. *American rough leaved Elm-Tree.*

This riſes to the height of about thirty feet, with a pretty ſtrong trunk; dividing into many branches, and covered with a lightiſh coloured rough bark. The leaves are oblong, oval and ſharp-pointed, ſomewhat unequally ſawed on their edges, unequal at the baſe, very rough on their upper ſurface and hairy underneath. The flowers are produced thick upon the branches, upon ſhort, collected footſtalks; and are ſucceeded by oval, compreſſed, membranaceous ſeed-veſſels, with entire margins; containing each one oval, compreſſed ſeed.

2. Ulmus mollifolia. *American ſoft-leaved Elm.*

This grows to the ſame ſize, or perhaps larger than the firſt kind. The leaves are of an oblong oval, ſharp-pointed, unequal at the baſe, doubly ſerrated on their edges and hairy underneath: but ſmooth on the upper ſurface, of thinner texture and ſofter than thoſe of the firſt kind. The ſeed-veſſels are alſo conſiderably ſmaller, end nicked or cleft, and ciliated or fringed on the margin.

VACCINIUM.

WHORTLE-BERRY.

Claſs 8. Order 1. Octandria Monogynia.

THE *Empalement* is very ſmall, above, and permanent.

The *Corolla* is of one petal, bell-ſhaped, and four-cleft: the diviſions turning back.

The *Filaments* are eight, ſimple. The *Antheræ* two-horned, furniſhed on the back with two ſpreading awns, and gaping at the tops.

The

The *Germen* is beneath. The *Style* ſimple, longer than the ſtamina. The *Stigma* obtuſe.
The *Seed-veſſel* a berry, globoſe, umbilicated and four cell'd.
The *Seeds* ſolitary and ſmall.
Obſ. The number of ſtamina are ten, in many of the ſpecies.

The Species, *with us, are,*

* *With annual deciduous leaves.*

1. VACCINIUM arboreum. *Winter, or Tree Whortle-Berry.*

This grows naturally in Carolina; riſing to the height of ten or fifteen feet, with a pretty ſtrong ſtem, dividing towards the top into many branches. The fruit is ſmall, ripening late in autumn.

2. VACCINIUM album. *Pennſylvanian White Whortle-berry.*

This is a ſmall ſhrub, riſing to the height of about two feet. The leaves are entire, egg-ſhaped and downy underneath. The flowers are produced at the ends of the branches, ſtanding two or three together upon very ſhort, naked footſtalks. The fruit is ſmall and whitiſh.

3. VACCINIUM corymboſum. *Cluſter-flowered Vaccinium.*

This grows naturally in ſwampy or moiſt places, riſing to the height of five or ſix feet. The leaves are entire, oblong, oval, and ſomewhat downy underneath. The flowers are produced in cluſters or rather one rowed, ſhort, roundiſh bunches; ſet pretty cloſe on the ſmall branches. The fruit is of a dark purpliſh colour when ripe, and of an agreeable acid taſte.

There

There are ſome varieties, I think, of this growing upon higher ground, and of much ſmaller growth; the leaves of ſome of which are moſt ſlightly and ſharply ſerrated.

4. VACCINIUM frondoſum. *Leafy Vaccinium, or Indian Gooſeberry.*

This grows naturally upon Whortle-berry ground; riſing to the height of three or four feet, generally with a leaning, crooked, branching ſtem. The leaves are entire and of an oval lance ſhape. The flowers are produced in frondoſe racemi or bunches, ſet with ſmall oblong leaves, at the boſom of which the flowers come out, upon pretty long, ſimple, ſlender footſtalks; they are ſomewhat bell-ſhaped, the antheræ are very long, two horned: the horns two cleft. The fruit or berries are oval, and of the ſize of a ſmall Gooſeberry; reddiſh coloured, ſoft, ſucculent, and of a diſagreeable taſte.

5. VACCINIUM liguſtrinum. *Privet-leaved Whortleberry.*

This riſes to the height of about two or three feet, dividing into ſmall branches. The leaves are ſmall and oblong. The flowers are produced in ſhort racemi, or bunches, which come out alternately, and thick upon the branches; and are naked, or without floral leaves. The berries are round, black and of an agreeable taſte.

6. VACCINIUM ſtamineum. *Long-leaved Vaccinium.*

This is alſo of ſmall growth. The leaves are oblong and very entire. The flowers come out at the boſom of the leaves, upon ſolitary, ſlender footſtalks, each

each ſupporting one flower, which is of a ſpreading bell-ſhape and five cleft at the border.

** *With evergreen leaves.*

7. Vaccinium hiſpidulum. *Marſh Vaccinium, or Cranberry.*

This grows naturally in moſſy ſwamps, with ſlender, creeping ſtalks, covered with briſtly ſcales. The leaves are oval, or ſomewhat oblong and ſhining. The fruit or berries are large and reddiſh coloured; and of a bitteriſh acid taſte.

8. Vaccinium pennſylvanicum. *Myrtle leaved Vaccinium, or Cranberry.*

The leaves of this are oval and ſharp pointed. The flowers are white and nodding, produced from the boſom of the leaves. The berries are red and ſmall,

VIRBURNUM.

PLIANT MEALLY, or WAY-FARING-TREE.

Claſs 5. Order 3. Pentandria Trigynia.

THE *Empalement* is four-toothed, above, very ſmall and permanent.

The *Corolla* is of one petal, bell-ſhaped, half five-cleſt: the diviſions obtuſe and reflexed.

The *Filaments* are five, awl-ſhaped and the length of the corolla. The *Antheræ* roundiſh.

The *Germen* beneath, roundiſh. The *Style* none, but in its place a top-ſhaped *Gland.* The *Stigmas* three.

The *Seed-veſſel,* a ſomewhat oval, compreſſed berry, of one cell.

The *Seed* one, hard, and of the ſame form.

The

The Species, *with us, are,*

1. VIBURNUM acerifolium. *Maple-leaved Viburnum.*

This riſes generally to the height of four or five feet, with an erect, ſlender ſtem, ſending off a few oppoſite branches. The leaves are ſomewhat three lobed, toothed, or pretty largely ſawed on their edges; a little hairy underneath, and joined to round footſtalks, placed oppoſite. The flowers terminate the ſtalks and branches in *cymæ* (about ſeven parted) or kind of umbels; they are white and are ſucceeded by ſomewhat oval, compreſſed, black berries when ripe.

2. VIBURNUM dentatum. *Toothed-leaved Viburnum, or Arrow Wood.*

This grows naturally in moiſt places, riſing up with ſeveral ſtraight ſtems, to the height of ten or twelve feet, ſending off ſeveral ſlender, oppoſite branches. The leaves are roundiſh or oval, pointed, and toothed on their edges, much veined and placed oppoſite, upon round, downy footſtalks. The flowers are produced at the tops of the ſtalks and branches, in *cymæ* or kind of umbels, about ſeven parted, in manner of thoſe of the Elder but much ſmaller; they are white and are ſucceeded by dark bluiſh coloured, oblong berries. The young ſhoots of this tree are generally uſed by the natives for arrows; whence it is known by the name of Arrow-wood.

3. VIBURNUM prunifolium. *Black Haw.*

This I take to be our common, ſmall black Haw; which riſes with a ſtiff ſtem to the height of about ten or fifteen feet, dividing into many branches, which

which are generally ſet pretty thick with ſhort, ſtrong, horizontal ſpurs or ſhort branches, ſtanding oppoſite. The bark of the trunk or ſtem is dark and rough, but of the young branches ſmooth. The leaves are of an oblong oval, ſmooth, finely and ſlightly ſerrated, and placed oppoſite upon channelled footſtalks. The flowers terminate the branches in four parted *cymæ*; they are white and make a pretty good appearance. The berries are oblong, oval, compreſſed and black when ripe.

4. VIBURNUM nudum. *Tinus leaved, or Swamp Viburnum.*

This grows naturally in moiſt or ſwampy places, riſing to the height of ten or twelve feet. The bark is ſmooth and of the young ſhoots purpliſh. The leaves are oval, lance-ſhaped, of a thick conſiſtence and lucid green colour: often ſlightly ſerrated, and ſtanding oppoſite. The flowers are produced in manner of the other kinds and are ſucceeded by berries of nearly the ſame ſize and ſhape, changing black when ripe.

5. VIBURNUM Lentago. *Canadian Viburnum.*

This riſes to the height of about ten or twelve feet, covered with a brown bark, and divided into many branches, which, when young, are covered with a ſmooth purpliſh bark. The leaves are ſmooth, oval, ſlightly ſawed on their edges, and ſtand generally oppoſite upon ſhort ſlender footſtalks. The flowers are produced in manner of the other kinds and are ſucceeded by berries of the ſame ſhape, and black when ripe.

6. VIBURNUM alnifolium. *Alder-leaved Viburnum.*

This grows naturally in Carolina and other parts of America; rising with a shrubby stalk to the height of eight or ten feet, covered with a smooth purplish bark, and divided into several branches. The leaves are heart-shaped, oval, sharp-pointed, deeply sawed on their edges, strongly veined, and placed opposite upon long slender footstalks. The flowers are collected in large cymes or umbels at the ends of the branches, those ranged on the border are male, but the center is filled with hermaphrodite flowers, which are succeeded by pretty large, oval berries, red coloured when ripe.

7. VIBURNUM triloba. *Mountain Viburnum.*

This grows naturally upon montains in the interior parts of Pennsylvania; rising with slender stems to the height of eight or ten feet. The leaves are somewhat like those of the Guelder Rose or Snow-ball tree; they are narrow at the base, but spreading and divided into three sharp-pointed lobes, the middle one largest, longest, and sometimes slightly toothed. The flowers are produced in form of the others, and are succeeded by berries of the same shape, of a pretty large size and red colour when ripe.

VISCUM.

MISSELTOE.

Class 22. Order 4. Dioecia Tetrandria.

* THE *Male* Flowers have their *Empalements*, five-parted; the leaves oval and equal.

They have no petals.

The *Filaments* or rather *Antheræ* are four, oblong and pointed, joined to the leaves of the calyx.

The

* The *Female* have *Empalements*, four leaved: the leaves oval, ſmall, ſitting cloſe, deciduous and placed upon the germen.
They have no petals.
The *Germen* are oblong, three-ſided, their margins crowned, obſolete, four-cleft, and beneath. The *Styles* none. The *Stigmas* obtuſe.
The *Seed-veſſels* berries, which are globoſe, ſmooth, and of of one cell.
The *Seeds* ſingle, ſomewhat heart-ſhaped, compreſſed and fleſhy.

The Species, *with us*, *are*,

1. Viscum rubrum. *Red berried Miſſeltoe.*

This grows upon the branches of trees and is not found growing in the earth as other plants. It riſes with ſlender woody ſtalks, ſeveral inches in height, ſpreading and forming a tuft or buſh. The leaves are lance-ſhaped and obtuſe. The flowers are produced in ſpikes from the ſides of the ſtalks, and thoſe of the female are ſucceeded by roundiſh red berries, containing each one heart-ſhaped, compreſſed ſeed, ſurrounded by a tough viſcid ſubſtance.

2. Viscum purpureum. *Purple-berried Miſſeltoe.*

This alſo riſes up from the branches of trees like the other. The leaves are inverſe-egg-ſhaped, or oval and narrowed towards the baſe. The flowers come out in *racemi* or bunches from the ſides of the ſtalks; the female of which are ſucceeded by berries of a purple colour when ripe.

There is a variety of this with yellow leaves, reſembling thoſe of the box; the berries are alſo produced in bunches and are of a ſnowy white when ripe.

Miſſeltoe is moſt frequently found growing upon the Nyſſa Sylvatica or Sour Gum, in the middle States, but to the ſouthward upon oaks. It is propagated by birds feeding upon the berries, the ſeeds of of which, ſometimes by their glutinoſity adhere to the outſide of their beaks, and are thus tranſported to neighbouring trees, and being wiped off upon their branches, ſtick faſt, and germinate, producing new plants. From the berries of Miſſeltoe, Birdlime was formerly made; but for this purpoſe thoſe of the common Holly are ſaid to be better. This plant hath been much recommended for the cure of Epilepſies.

VITIS.

The VINE.

Claſs 5. Order 1. Pentandria Monogynia.

THE *Empalement* is five toothed and very ſmall.

The *Petals* are five, rude, ſmall, and falling off.

The *Filaments* are five, awl-ſhaped, a little ſpreading, and falling off. The *Antheræ* are ſimple.

The *Germen* ovate. The *Style* none. The *Stigma* obtuſe-headed.

The *Seed-veſſel* a berry, roundiſh, large, and of one cell.

The *Seeds* are five, hard, end-bitten at one end, and contracted at the other.

The Species, *with us, are,*

1. VITIS arborea. *Carolinian Vine, or Pepper-Tree.*

This grows naturally in Carolina, riſing with ſlender, ligneous, climbing ſtalks, and faſtening themſelves by tendrils to any neighbouring ſupport. The leaves are branching and winged, compoſed generally of two ſide branches of five leaves each, two of three leaves, and terminating with three; which are ſmall and ſomewhat toothed. The flowers are produced in looſe cluſters from the wings of the ſtalks; they

they are ſmall and white, and are ſucceeded by ſmall berries of a purpliſh colour when ripe.

2. VITIS vinifera americana. *American Grape Vine.*

There are many varieties of this, which generally riſe up with ſtrong ſtems, climbing by tendrils or claſpers upon neighbouring trees for ſupport, often to the height of thirty or forty feet, and of two, three or four inches in diameter; covered with a dark, rough, looſe bark. The leaves are generally heart-ſhaped and ſomewhat three lobed; ſawed on their edges, and downy or hairy underneath. The grapes are produced in bunches, in form of the European kinds, generally between the ſize of a Currant and Gooſeberry: darkiſh coloured, or with a light bluiſh caſt, and for the moſt part of an acid agreeable taſte.

3. VITIS vulpina. *Fox-Grape Vine.*

This in manner of growth hath much the appearance of the other kinds. The leaves are generally larger, and ſmooth, but whitiſh underneath. The fruit or grapes are about the ſize of a common cherry and have a ſtrong ſcent, a little approaching to that of a Fox, whence the name of Fox-grape. There are alſo varieties of this, ſome with whitiſh or reddiſh fruit which is generally moſt eſteemed, and others with black, of which are our largeſt grapes.

4. VITIS Labruſca. *Wild American Vine.*

The ſtems of this have the appearance of our other kinds. The leaves are generally leſs and of a thinner

thinner texture. The berries or grapes are produced in loose bunches; they are small, and are of several kinds, some reddish, others of a shining black, and some of a bluish colour; all of an acerb disagreeable taste.

5. VITIS laciniosa. *Canadian Parsley-leaved Vine.*

The stalks and branches of this resemble the others. The leaves are cut into many slender segments, somewhat in manner of a Parsley-leaf. The grapes are round and white, and are produced in loose bunches; they are late ripe and not very well flavoured.

XANTHOXYLUM.

The TOOTH-ACH TREE.

Class 22. Order 5. Dioecia Pentandria.

* THE *Male* Flowers have *Empalements* four-parted; the leaves oval, erect and coloured.

They have no *Petals*.

The *Filaments* in each are generally five, awl-shaped, erect and longer than the calyx. The *Antheræ* are twin, roundish and furrowed.

* The *Female* have *Empalements* as the male.

They have no *Petals*.

The *Germen* in each are generally five, often less, with short footstalks, oval and ending in as many awl-shaped *Styles*. The *Stigmas* are obtuse.

The *Seed-vessels* are *Capsules*, of the same number with the germen, oblong, of one cell and two valves.

The *Seeds* are single, roundish and smooth.

The

The Species, *with us,*

XANTHOXYLUM fraxinifolium. *Ash-leaved Tooth-ach Tree.*

This grows naturally in Pennſylvania and Maryland; riſing with a pretty ſtrong ſtem to the height of ten or twelve feet; and dividing in many branches, which are covered with a purpliſh bark, and armed at each bud with two ſtrong, ſharp ſpines. The leaves are compoſed of four or five pair of lobes, terminated by an odd one; which are entire and of an oblong egg-ſhape, placed oppoſite and ſitting cloſe to the common footſtalk, which is alſo ſet with a few ſpines underneath. The flowers are produced along the branches, upon ſhort collected footſtalks; and thoſe of the female are each ſucceeded, for the moſt part, with five diſtinct, oval capſules, joined by ſhort footſtalks to the common receptacle, and ſpreading above; each containing one roundiſh, ſmooth ſeed.

There is ſaid to be another Species, or perhaps Variety, of this in South Carolina, differing in having the lobes of their leaves lance-ſhaped, ſawed on their edges and having footſtalks. The bark and capſules are of a hot acrid taſte, and are uſed for eaſing the tooth-ach, from whence it obtained the name of Tooth-ach Tree: a tincture of them are alſo much commended for the cure of the Rheumatiſm.

XANTHORHIZA.

SHRUB YELLOW ROOT.

Claſs 5. Order 6. Pentandria Polygynia.

THE *Empalement* none.

The *Corolla* is of five petals, lance-ſhaped, pointed and ſpreading.

The

The *Nectarium* crowning the corolla, of five ſmall leaves, ſomewhat two-lobed: the lobes very ſmall, roundiſh, or rather runcinate, and inſerted by ſlender claws in the common receptacle, alternating with the petals.

The *Filaments* five, ſhort and thread-form. The *Antheræ* roundiſh.

The *Germen* ſeveral, moſt frequently from ſeven to eleven, ſmall and ending in as many awl-ſhaped, ſhort, incurved *Styles*. The *Stigmas* acute.

The *Seed-veſſels* as many Capſules; which are ſmall, ſomewhat oval, compreſſed, oblique pointed, of one cell and two valves, joined at their baſe to the common receptacle, and ſpreading above.

The *Seeds* are ſingle in each cell, ſmall, ſomewhat ovate and lightly compreſſed

Obſ. The petals are ſometimes ſix in number. The number of Stamina are alſo ſometimes increaſed.

The Species *but one*, viz.

XANTHORHIZA ſimpliciſſima. *Shurb Yellow Root.*

This is a ſmall ſhrub, growing naturally in Carolina. The roots are ſlender and cylindrical, but ſending off ſide ſhoots by which it ſpreads much; the wood of which, together with that of the ſtems, are of a bright yellow colour. The ſtems are ſlender, riſing to the height of two feet or more, generally ſimple, or without branches, and covered with a lightiſh brown bark. The leaves are compound, conſiſting of two pair of oppoſite lobes, terminated by an odd one; the lobes are much and deeply cut or cleft on their edges, (ſomewhat in form of Garden Lovage) and joined to very long, common footſtalks, coming out from the tops of the ſtems. The flowers are produced at the top of the former year's growth, in a compound or panicled *racemus*; having their partial footſtalks generally three flowered; they

are

are ſmall and purpliſh coloured, and are ſucceeded by little heads of ſmall, compreſſed capſules, each encloſing one ſmall ſeed. The flowers on the partial or ſmall footſtalks, are not produced at once, thoſe that are middle-moſt or terminal come out firſt and are hermaphrodite, and generally barren; thoſe on the ſides come out later, but one of which is generally fruitful; from whence, I had ſuppoſed, ſome of the flowers were female, and to the contrary of which I am not yet fully convinced.

This ſhrub, from the yellowneſs of its roots and ſtems, it is highly probable, might be employed to good purpoſe in dying cloaths, &c. It has hitherto been undeſcribed by Botanical writers, though named in ſome late Catalogues in honour of M. Marbois; but having impoſed the former name, before I had heard of this, have choſe to retain it as being expreſſive of its qualities and appearance.

ADVERTISEMENT.

BOXES of SEEDS, and growing PLANTS, of the FOREST TREES, FLOWERING SHRUBS, &c. of the American United States; are made up in the beſt manner and at a reaſonable rate by the Author. All Orders in this line, directed for *Humphry Marſhall*, of Cheſter County, Pennſylvania; to the Care of Dr. THOMAS PARKE, in Philadelphia, will be carefully and punctually attended to.

INDEX *of* LATIN GENERIC NAMES.

INDEX *of* ENGLISH NAMES.

Fern,

Pavia,

www.ingramcontent.com/pod-product-compliance
Lightning Source LLC
Chambersburg PA
CBHW030837270326
41928CB00007B/1095

* 9 7 8 3 3 3 7 2 2 5 7 3 5 *